WOMAN
Incognito

WOMAN
Incognito

TRANSSEXUAL WITHOUT TRANSITION

Transcender Lee

OVERSOUL PRESS

Published by Oversoul Press

Manufactured in the United States of America

FIRST EDITION

Cover and book design by Barbara Aronica-Buck for Booktrix

Paperback ISBN: 978-0-9968919-0-5
eBook ISBN: 978-0-9968919-1-2

Names used for people in this book are not their real names, with the exception of a few authors, political candidates, or other public figures.

This book is dedicated to
my wife and my four children.

ACKNOWLEDGMENTS

I wish to acknowledge the invaluable help of "Dr. Flanagan" and "Dr. Cohen," who assisted me so much in the process of discovering, accepting, and living with my true gender identity.

CONTENTS

CHAPTER I

EARLY GLIMPSES?

It was 1967 and Aretha Franklin was the Queen of Soul and I did not know why her song "A Natural Woman" drilled straight into my soul. I told a friend that listening to her was very rough for me. He asked me why, and I did not know the answer. I was twenty-five. Three decades later, I finally understood that when Aretha sang the words "You make me feel like a natural woman," she made *me* feel like a natural woman.

This book is the story of two paths I have taken during my life. The first was a tortuous path to self-discovery. The second is the path I have been following since I realized that I am a woman in a male body. That second path began in my mid-fifties, and it is a fascinating adventure. My hope is that my story may prove of some value to some of the other people who are struggling to make sense of their own gender identities and figure out how to live with those identities.

The story may actually begin before I was born. In fact, it may begin when my mother was born. She was the youngest child in her family and had five older brothers. According to my father, my grandmother had always wanted a girl, but when it finally happened, she could not believe it. In fact, when the doctor said, "It's a girl," she supposedly replied, "That's all right, doctor, you don't have to humor me."

Did my mother also want a daughter? It would seem likely enough. Before me, she had only boys. My two brothers were just three years apart, and I have been told that she had lost a child between them. Close spacing seems to have been the game plan. But I was not born for another seven years. Had my mother, like her own mother, wanted a daughter but become resigned to never having one? If so, her perhaps unexpected pregnancy might have given her new hope. And if she did hope that I would be a girl, could that have influenced the way she began to raise me when I was very young? Nothing she did could have ultimately affected my gender, but it could have affected how I experienced my childhood.

Of course this is all speculation, but I do remember an intriguing incident. My mother related to me a story she had heard or read about a boy whose mother had raised him as a girl for several years. I am not sure whether she was telling just me, or the whole family, but I only remember the two of us being present. Why did she tell me? Did the idea appeal to her? Did she wonder whether it would appeal to me?

Whether or not my mother's hopes or actions had anything to do with it, I have a very strong feeling that at a very early age I sensed on some level that I was really a girl. But sometime while I was still very young, it was somehow communicated to me that I could not be a girl, was not *allowed* to be a girl, and would have to accept being a boy. The message was probably initiated by my family, reinforced in school, and strengthened by every aspect of society that I encountered. I cannot blame my parents, my brothers, or anyone else. There was hardly any real understanding of gender at that time, and they were simply expressing what an entire culture had told *them*. It was a message I would continue to receive, over and over, in countless ways, year after year after year. If you have a penis, you are a boy. Period. End of story.

Except, of course, it would not turn out to be my story. Over the last several years of therapy, I have become convinced that when you delve into the past there will always be some things that you can never know for sure. In those cases, it can be very useful to construct a story that is at least plausible, and consistent with what you do know. Many of the thoughts, feelings, and experiences that I am going to recount may well be experienced by other people without meaning they are transsexual. But I am not writing about other people. I am writing about *my own* experiences, and how they seem to fit together in my story. I do not claim that any one of these experiences meant that I was transsexual, but I do feel that, taken together, they are part of my transsexual story.

For openers, let me introduce you to some of my childhood heroes. Actually, they were heroines. That in itself may have been unusual for a boy, which I and everyone else thought I was. Both then and now, my favorite superhero is Wonder Woman. She was awesome! Smart, athletic, and what is now called "eye candy." But there was more to it than that. She was also self-sufficient, with no apparent need to rely on men for anything. Could that have been part of her appeal for me?

Although I was not aware of it at the time, looking back I have to think I may have unconsciously begun to wish that the girl hidden within me could become independent of the male externals. Is that reaching? Very possibly, but I am not a psychologist and do not pretend to be. I am just a woman looking for a way to make sense of my experiences to myself.

If Wonder Woman was the confident equal of any man, another childhood heroine of mine made a conscious effort to be *better* than a man. Her name was Annie Oakley, but I knew her from my parents' record album of the Broadway hit *Annie Get Your Gun*. As a young child, I loved the song "Anything You Can Do." How many young boys would love a song about a woman doing everything better than a man? And does the phallic symbolism of "gun" have significance? Was Annie, at least metaphorically, being portrayed as a woman with a penis? Either way, she was clearly challenging gender stereotypes. Although the thought of that Annie (there will be another) possessing a penis requires an inference, the idea pops up quite explicitly in another childhood memory.

For a very long time, I have been aware of a childhood dream that had always puzzled me. I think I always felt there must have been a reason for it but could not get a handle on it. I had to be at least six, because it was set in the small Virginia town my family moved to from Minnesota when I was that age. I was in the schoolyard at my elementary school, in a portion of it that seemed somewhat remote from the school building and the main part of the playground. Of course the distance is probably greatly exaggerated in my mind. Anyway, I came into that area, and there was a girl there whom I either knew a little or had at least seen around my church. She may, in fact, have been the same one who once derided me for crying at church school. There in the playground, she showed me her penis. By then I must have known that girls did not have penises. My interpretation now is that the dream was telling me that a girl *could* have one. In other words, that I might be a girl even though I had one. And, if everyone in a dream is really oneself, was I actually showing myself a picture of me as what I actually was, a girl with a penis? At the very least, this interpretation finally makes sense of something that I could not understand before, and in a way that fits into the bigger picture as I now see it.

I also have a number of memories of the playground that really happened. Several of them have a common theme: myself as a willing victim. One of those memories is about a sort of game with two boys whom I considered friends. During recess, we would go over to a bank of earth just across a road at the edge of the playground. They would take me to the top and tell me to slide down it. The problem was that it was always muddy. So much so that we named it the "Muddy Slide." It must have made an incredible mess of my pants. The whole thing was basically harmless, but I have to ask myself why I was always the one who had to slide in the mud, especially since there were other similar incidents.

Another example of me in the role of victim took place on the other side of the playground, which was bordered by a little creek. Apparently the edges of the

playground were popular for activities that were on the
edge of respectability. A bunch of boys often spent recess
down by the creek, and for a while I went down there
with them. I do not remember what we did there except
for a couple of times when the others tied my hands
together and treated me as a prisoner. After the first time,
one of them pretended to be on my side and asked me
if I had any secrets.

I fell for it, and showed him a way to hold your
wrists when they are being tied together that makes it
easy to get your hands out of the rope. He was obviously
a spy, because the next time they made sure I could not
use that trick. And to add insult to injury, the following
day the same boy asked me again if I had any secrets.
Willing victim or not, I was not dumb enough to make
the same mistake again, and that was the end of that
game. Still, I had once again been cast in the role of victim. I guess it was typecasting. And that was not my last
part in the continuing drama.

The next scene must have been the most humiliating. There was a back door to the school and some sort
of outside staircase. One day a group of boys held me
while some of them went up the stairs to a landing that
was just above my head. And then they literally spat on
me. Over and over. On my face. My glasses were
streaked with saliva. Why did things like that keep happening to me? I can only think that I must have exuded
an aura of vulnerability.

Boys were not supposed to be vulnerable. They were
supposed to be tough. They were supposed to fight back.
Strong, not weak. Active, not passive. Girls could be
passive. They could follow rather than lead. Did I

subconsciously think that I belonged in the girls' stereotype rather than the boys'? Although I cannot know for
sure what was going on in my subconscious at the age
of nine or ten, this theory seems plausible and fits into
my developing story.

Fortunately, not all of my playground memories are
so grim. For example, there was the time some boys were
picking up sides to play basketball and one of them recommended me. His words were, "He don't look good,
but he is." I was pretty good for my age, as he knew
because I had actually taught him to play. But although
it felt good to be praised by a boy in front of other boys,
most of my positive experiences on the playground were
with girls.

I remember hanging around with girls in the area
where the swings, seesaws, and jungle gym were located.
One time I was asking some of them for dares, mainly
to show that I liked them. I did like girls a lot, and I told
myself that I had a precocious interest in them when
most boys still preferred to hang out with each other.
Now I think I was attracted to girls at that age largely
because I wanted to be one of them.

There was one little girl whom I especially liked
hanging around with. I will call her Alice, but like most
of the people I write about in this book, that is not her
real name. She deserves more than a little space, but I
will start by using her to finish up the playground theme.
At some point, probably fourth grade, she and I and a
couple of other kids used to spend most of recess on the
jungle gym. We would climb around on it a little, but
mostly we used it as a sort of clubhouse. Another member of that little "club" was a boy who also hung out with

us at a class roller-skating party. He greatly impressed us with what we called his "scooter stroke." He would keep one skate on the floor and push himself along with the other one. That made him a real speed demon.

The bond between Alice and me went far beyond jungle gym and roller-skating. Being among the few Catholics in our class made us *de facto* members of what was virtually a secret society. The religious difference between us and our classmates was emphasized once a week, when some woman came in to teach the Bible. (Yes, there was Bible class in a public school back then.) Since the Catholic Church viewed it as a *Protestant* class, Catholics were excused. As well as I can recall, there were only three of us and we spent the time in the library. The librarian was a sort of den mother to us, and one time she sent away for a bag of stamps for a dollar and we each put in a quarter. All of us were interested in stamp collecting, which further strengthened our club-like connection.

Looking back, I find my relationship with Alice very interesting. We were never boyfriend and girlfriend or anything like that. I could say we were just friends, but I feel that there was more to it than that. As I see it now, we were more like sisters. One day at church while we were standing in line for the confessional, we wrote our names several times in the dust on the wall. My brother Frank saw it later and thought we were linking our names in a boy-girl sort of way, but that was not it. It was more as though we were recording the fact that we belonged in the same place because of some other kind of bond. Sisterhood. When she wanted to make a buzzer for a science project, she called me up to ask how. When a local shop was selling chameleons, we both showed up at school wearing them on our clothes. Mine spent the day under my shirt collar with only its tail hanging out.

When my family moved away, Alice and I exchanged a letter or two. After that, we had no contact until our junior year in high school, when her family too was living in another state. I saw her again when we had both just started college. Our schools were not far apart, so I called her up and took her to dinner. It was sort of a date and sort of not a date. The main thing I remember is that she spoke with a pronounced southern drawl. I asked her why, saying that she had never talked like that when we lived in the south. She replied, "I know, but the boys up here love it!" We enjoyed seeing each other, but there was still no romantic spark or anything. Our paths have not crossed since then.

My relationship with another girl I knew in grade school was not sisterly. Maggie and I professed love to each other in the third or fourth grade and were boyfriend and girlfriend on and off into college. We were academic rivals, and rather than causing hostility, our competition made us feel that we shared something special at the top of our class. Actually, most of the girls and women with whom I have had close relationships have been very intelligent. Although I have heard that most boys and many men do not want a female to be as smart as them, I have preferred the ones who are. But of course I never was a boy, which could explain why I had a different attitude toward girls. That explanation would fit in with many experiences I shall be relating in my story of growing up transsexual.

Maggie and I danced together, played Ping-Pong

together, shot baskets together, sledded together, and walked home together. By the eighth grade I was chasing after other girls, but I was never really infatuated with another girl for several more years.

Although my interest in some girls seems to me to have grown out of my desire to *be* a girl, my attraction to Maggie was like that of a boy to a girl or, in my case, of a lesbian girl to another girl. My attraction to girls was what was expected of a boy. And it was only one typically boyish interest of mine. Actually, I had many of them. I loved toy guns, and from them I graduated to a BB gun and finally a real .22 rifle. Not satisfied with guns, I also had a bow and shot arrows all over the place. I liked knives and had a collection of them. One of them was a so-called "Malayan throwing knife," with which I made a total mess of the back door to the garage. (Until I compiled this list, it never occurred to me how many phallic symbols little boys like to accumulate!)

In addition to playing with assorted weapons, I played neighborhood football, baseball, and basketball. And was sorry that restrictions on my physical activity (due to a congenital heart condition) kept me from playing Little League baseball or other organized competitive sports. Another usually male interest I had back then, and which I shared with the boy across the street, was radio and electronics. Later on, in high school, we both got ham radio licenses.

I also had a skill that, in an odd way, ended up making me both one of the boys and one of the girls. I was quite a good speller and had a record of winning most of the spelling bees in our class. I am not sure I paid much attention to the gender of my competitors until one day when we were playing boys against girls. Then it became obvious that the best spellers were mostly girls. In fact, it got down to five girls and me. Then, in the words of one boy, I "mowed them down," and carried the day for the boys. So there I was, excelling at spelling along with the girls and being hailed as a hero by the boys!

I actually do not recall doing many things that are generally associated with girls. But there were a few incidents that may suggest some gender ambivalence. For example, one day I was showing a friend various things in my room and took out a toy iron. He immediately said, "That's a girl's toy. All your toys are girls' toys." I don't know what other toys he meant, but whatever he meant, he was clearly telling me that I did not meet gender expectations.

The remark about toys illustrates how other people sometimes perceived me as being like a girl in some way. There were also times when I deliberately tried to be like a girl. I remember a couple of times when I pretended that I was dressed as a girl. I really liked the way the girls in my class smoothed their skirts before sitting own. Wishing that I could do that, I tried it with my pants, but quickly realized that it did not work with them. Another time, some of the neighborhood boys and I pretended to actually wear a piece of girls' clothing. Someone had shown one of them how to tie up a T-shirt to make it look more like a bra or something of the sort. We all thought it was funny.

I remember only one time in my childhood when I put on any clothing that was really intended for a girl or woman. It was a piece of my mother's underwear, and all I remember is that it was pink and too big for me. I also remember only one time that I tried to look more like a girl physically. I was with another boy and I tucked my genitals between my legs and asked, "Doesn't that look like a girl?" He answered, very unenthusiastically, that yes, it looked like a girl. He did not seem to think much of the idea of a boy *wanting* to look like a girl.

Once, a teacher wanted me to do something more boyish than what I had in mind. It was the end of my eighth-grade year and we were all asked to fill out a form indicating what courses we wanted to take the following year. Although I already knew that we were moving to another state, I filled it out anyway. Later on, the teacher informed me that I would be the only freshman boy in the dramatics class. I said that in that case I would not take it. Apparently that was what she wanted to hear, because she launched into telling me that she wanted me to do things with other boys. Like woodworking. That seems ironic to me, since I believe she was the same one who had previously asked me to play the only male role in a play called something like *The Old Maids' Club*. Talk about mixed messages!

Something else I received mixed messages about in my childhood was religion and spirituality. Such things have always been important parts of my life, and their influence on me definitely began at an early age. My mother considered the Catholic Church to be the source of all authority. She insisted that we follow its every rule and then some. There was a rule that you had to go to church for Mass every Sunday and "Holy Day of Obligation." But here was a loophole. When on vacation, if you were more than twenty-five miles from the nearest church, you did not have to go. We were, but we did.

The Church was the ultimate authority, and for me the Church was embodied in my mother. This state of affairs was difficult for my father, who had been raised Methodist and became an Episcopalian but was not really a religious person. His views on faith and morals simply did not seem relevant in the little theocracy of our family. I once actually referred to him as a pagan, not as an insult but simply as what I thought was a fact.

There were two parish priests while we lived in that town. I thought of them as "stern priest" and "cheerful priest." Cheerful priest came after stern priest, and my father actually seemed a bit scandalized at my delight when I saw in the morning paper that stern priest was leaving. But I cannot blame myself: stern priest had seen me after summer vacation and declared, in front of my friends, "Skinny hasn't gained an ounce!" And surely my judgment was vindicated when cheerful priest rewarded all of us altar boys after the Christmas service by giving us "pictures of Thomas Jefferson" that turned out to be two-dollar bills bearing that President's image. My positive and negative feelings about our different parish priests also apply to other experiences I had as a Catholic kid.

I think my most positive experience was being an altar boy. That made me feel directly involved in the most important rituals of the Church, but it also makes me understand how not being allowed to do the same thing made my wife feel *excluded*. Part of that experience was learning and reciting the Latin responses during the Mass. The Latin contributed to my sense that I was part of an elite group within the Church. That was one of many things in my childhood that told me that being male determined a person's role in life and even made you superior to females.

The two most negative experiences of religion that I remember from my boyhood both pertained to religious instruction classes. Grade school level classes were held on Saturday rather than Sunday, because Catholic children were expected to attend the Sunday morning services with their parents. In general, I suppose, that was not too bad, even though it took away our Saturday mornings, when other kids were out playing. But one morning it was a nightmare. Whatever the reason, perhaps because I had forgotten one of the many prayers or catechism answers we had to learn, I suddenly burst into tears. That was humiliating in itself, and one of the girls made it even worse by expressing her scorn.

Eventually some other kids and I got the priest to let us go to the Monday evening class with the high school students. That was more interesting, but one night I was late and was so afraid to go in that I would not get out of the car. My father drove me back home, but made some derogatory remark about a religion that scared children so much. And indeed, at least for me, fear did seem to be a very strong part of Catholicism. Of course, the ultimate fear was that of going to hell for breaking one of God's laws (or even just one of the Church's rules). I am not saying that everyone has felt that way. As throughout this book, I am speaking only of my own experience. Even for me, my religion would become more multi-faceted during my high school years.

CHAPTER II

LIFE AS A BRAIN

I have always suspected that the real reason we moved from our little Southern town to a major Midwestern city was that my parents had taken a public stand on the subject of school integration. They were in favor of it and that was not a popular position in that time and place. One of my father's friends told him, "We will never let this happen."

Although it turned out that they could not stop it, by then we were ensconced north of the Mason-Dixon line. Whatever the basic reason for moving, one factor in the timing may have been the choice of a high school for me. I think I wanted to go to the same prestigious New England prep school that my brother Sam had attended, but my mother seemed determined that I go to a Catholic school. She started talking about an almost equally prestigious Catholic prep school and soon I wanted to go there. But then my father said, "There's another one. " The other one turned out to be a relatively new and relatively unknown school in the city he seemed to want to live in anyway. And since more than half of its students were day students, if we moved there I would be able to live at home.

That seemed to seal the deal, so we made plans to

move there; and my parents took me to the school to apply for admission. We found that the freshman class for that fall was already full, but I was given a couple of tests, and we were told they would let us know if there would be room for me. We bought a lovely house on a lake, and then went north to the bigger lake where we had a summer cabin. In Minnesota, "the land of 10,000 lakes," it seemed that almost everyone went to "the cabin on the lake" in the summer.

When we made the actual move at the end of the summer, I still did not know whether I was about to go to the private Catholic school or the local public school. Then a letter arrived from the former. I tore it open and found out that I was accepted. One way or another, a place in the freshman class had been found for me. I was very excited as we made various preparations and bought my books and gym suits. I also paid fifty cents to a senior for a "canteen pass," which I later learned was fictitious. When my mother took me to school the first day, I was filled with great expectations.

The day did not go quite as I expected. I got lost in the corridors and arrived at history class a minute or two late. Brother Matthew closed the door in my face, saying, "Get out of my classroom." I did have enough sense to go to the school office and explain my plight to the headmaster, who walked back to the classroom with me and explained to the good brother that I had just been a bit confused. So was it to be good brother and bad brother now? Actually, Brother Matthew calmed down after a week or two and became one of my favorite teachers, though we did get another taste of his temper later in the year. The rest of the morning went somewhat better, but then in the afternoon the physical education teacher put us through a course of calisthenics that I think was grueling for all of us.

Sore and exhausted, when I got home I sadly told my parents that I did not think I liked my new school. My father, who had observed many freshman classes during his teaching career, wisely assured me that I could not tell anything from the first day. Sure enough, I soon learned to love the school that would be pretty much the center of my universe for the next four years. Especially since my academic success was clearly signaled by my 4.0 average in the first grading period. That caught even me by surprise, since our English teacher had declared that he never gave an "A" to a freshman.

The Rubicon had been crossed. My high school identity was established. I was a brain. The smartest kid in the class. And, of course, the one who must never get a "B"; both an honor and a burden. By the end of the year I had definitely decided that I would be valedictorian. I think I felt the weight of that expectation not only at school but also at home. I now had the responsibility of living up to my family's academic standards. It was a high bar. My father had a Ph.D. and, although he was now retired, until then the college where he taught English had always seemed to be a part of our identity. My mother had an M.A. in English and had been state president of the American Association of University Women at a time when being a college graduate was still a considerable distinction for a woman. Sam had recently graduated from an Ivy League college and was doing graduate work, also in English, at a highly respected west coast university. The expectation was that he, like dad, would soon have a Ph.D., although he changed his mind after receiving an M.A. and became a high school English teacher. Does anyone sense a pattern here?

It does seem that my family's academic focus was very narrow. English came first, then the other humanities, and then pretty much a wasteland. At one point, I veered away from what seems to me to have been my expected path. I remember telling Sam, probably in the eighth grade, that I was going to be an electronic engineer, and electronics was definitely my main hobby. But by high school, I was mostly back on track and accepted the idea that my strength was in the humanities and not in math and science. That was probably why I did not take chemistry, even though the previous year I had the highest score on a standardized biology test and would do so again in physics the following year. I also did not take calculus, perhaps because for two grading periods in second-year algebra I had received the only "Bs" I got in high school. I suppose that lent some credibility to the "not good in math" theory, though the fact remains that all in all I did do fairly well even in that subject. And, to add to the confusion, my senior year SAT scores in English and math were almost identical. Maybe I was starting to catch on, because I began talking about perhaps majoring in astronomy. But my father, undaunted, told me that was not a good idea because I was not good at things like that. And, once again, I bought it. I still could not let go of what other people thought I was, and be what I thought I was.

Along with its emphasis on academic excellence, my family placed a very high value on intelligence. And it was apparently assumed that the two always went together. Although initially I accepted that equation, by the end of high school I had developed a somewhat different outlook. I clearly remember telling Sam which student I considered to be the second most brilliant member of my class. (Yes. I assumed I was the first. Modesty was not my strong suit.) Sam, who was by then teaching at the school l attended and had actually taught both of us, said he had not seen any evidence of it. I must have seen something he missed, because the boy in question went on to become a great success in business and, interestingly, an influential trustee of a large university. The fact is that he had graduated high in our class and done well at a major Catholic university. But I think his leaning was always in the direction of business, in which Sam never had an interest.

That conversation was perhaps the beginning of a decades' long process through which I have come to understand that there are many types of intelligence, which are manifested in many different ways. I now appreciate the talents and knowledge possessed by countless people who never excelled at formal education. A few years ago I told an employee that he was much smarter than he thought. He replied, "Well, I'm not school smart." Precisely. He had bought into a narrow concept of intelligence that had for a long time caused him to underestimate the vast amount of knowledge that he had acquired and learned how to utilize, outside of any formal educational setting. The same thing can be said, indeed, about my brother Frank, who ventured off the family's well-beaten academic path to develop interests and abilities that I admire much more than he may realize.

The high value placed on a rather narrowly defined

type of intelligence may have been only one aspect of a general feeling that certain people are naturally superior to others. In fact, I think that in some ways I was raised to be a snob, but ultimately it did not take. My father seemed to have a strong belief that there were different classes of people, some being superior to others. And it seemed clear that he thought he belonged to an inherently superior class. He used to speak of what he called a "reverse social revolution" in which a natural aristocracy would regain its rightful elevated status over a willingly subservient lower class. I think Sam expressed a dim view of that idea, but at the time I probably shared my father's attitude and assumed that I was entitled by nature to be in the privileged class. My mother expressed things more graciously, but coming from a family that had more than its share of successful people, I think she may have had a sense of *noblesse oblige.*

Whatever sense of superiority I may have had, it was in conflict with a desire to fit in. One time I was in the school smoker and one of the other boys noticed that I was not inhaling. He asked me why I bothered even smoking at all, and a third boy said, "to be one of the boys." He did not know how right he was and neither did I. But being one of the boys, literally, was exactly what I was trying to do, and what I would never be able to do.

Most people seem to feel a strong need to conform, to be like others, to live in accordance with prevailing social standards. This is part of why it is so difficult for transsexuals to accept their deviation from social norms. I have always felt a tension between wanting to conform and wanting not to conform. And yet, the very act of rejecting the standards and expectations of the majority can make one feel like part of a minority. One of my college roommates expressed it very well. When I told him I was a nonconformist, he said, "like all the other nonconformists." It was a good point. I think the need to fit in someplace is so strong that people who do not fit in look for others like themselves so as to have some group they belong to. Adolescents commonly do this to establish their own identity by embracing a culture different from that of adults. But since I did not know what made me different from the others, there was no subculture I could turn to for acceptance. Not feeling comfortable anywhere else, I tended to identify with adults, their culture, and their values more than most people do at that age. When I did start to challenge that culture, I did it in a chaotic, disoriented, and sometimes extremist way.

For me, the biggest question about conforming to social values would pertain to expected gender roles. During my high school years, I was bombarded by gender stereotypes from every direction. To begin with, my school itself was a male bastion. Not only was it a school for boys only, but it was run by a religious order of "brothers" who had chosen a lifestyle lived in all-male religious communities. In addition, although not all of the teachers were brothers, they were all male. And of course, as Catholics, both the students and the brothers subscribed to the idea that the Church should be run by an all-male priesthood. Having said that, I hasten to add that nothing in this book is meant to denigrate any religion or denomination. As will become clear later, I respect them all as valid spiritual paths.

Within that vigorously male-oriented scholastic setting, I received many messages stressing that men and

women had very different and often unequal roles. I
think my favorite example was a declaration by my Latin
teacher to the effect that the basic source of America's
ills was the fact that husbands were washing the dishes.
I remember that at the beginning of my first marriage I
thought, much to my embarrassment now, that I should
stay out of the kitchen. Now where could I have gotten
an idea like that? Another doozie was provided by a good
friend who was also my academic counterpart in the class
ahead of me. I do not remember how the subject came
up, but he stated that a woman cannot be an intellectual.
I countered that I knew a woman who was one. Unflus-
tered, he responded, "Then she isn't really a woman!" I
can only hope he changed his mind before he became a
psychiatrist.

Another instance, certainly not as outrageous but
more significant for me personally, came from my
brother Sam. It was the day after I played the title role
in Shakespeare's *Henry IV, Part I,* which Sam had
directed. My mother related that another mother had
told her that I had beautiful hands. Sam immediately
interjected, "Boys don't like to hear that." But I *did* like
it. So without knowing it, he was saying there must be
something wrong with me. After all, the only alternative
would be that I was not a boy.

In the context of that same play, Sam had already
said something even more fraught with unintended
meaning. That story begins a few years earlier, when my
parents and I saw the play at the Stratford, Ontario,
Shakespeare Theater. I liked it and I loved the character
of Prince Hal, the heir apparent to the throne. He was
everything I thought I wanted to be: dashing, funny,

heroic, and destined for greatness. From that day on, I wanted to play that part. And when, after all that time, Sam announced that he had chosen that play to direct at school, I thought I would really get the chance. But then came the auditions. I read for several parts and told Sam which one I wanted. But he said I just had to face facts about myself. What he meant was that my skinny, underweight appearance would just not be credible in that role. Fair enough. Directors have to make that kind of decision. That was not the big problem. The big problem was that he was also saying that my body would keep me from being something I desperately wanted to be. At the time, of course, neither of us knew what that was. It would be decades before even I would know that it was not a medieval prince, but a woman.

Not all of the incidents I remember from those years were about someone else imposing stereotypes upon me. At least one time that I recall, I was the one limiting myself with a stereotype, and someone else tried to set me free. When I was a junior in high school, my father was stricken with a heart attack while attending meetings in New York. When a friend of his could not contact him, the friend got the hotel staff to enter my dad's room, and they found him on the floor. He was rushed to the hospital and was kept there for a couple of weeks. That was when an understanding of the relationship between heart trouble and cholesterol was just being developed, and there were all sorts of conflicting theories going around. My Easter vacation was just beginning, so I was able to go to New York with my mother to be with my father.

Knowing that my old friend Alice was now living in

New Jersey, my mother and I took a bus out to see her family.

It was really good to see Alice again. Most of my closest relationships have always been with girls or women, whether just friends or something more. Looking back, I think that this strong affinity for females reflected both sexual attraction to them and emotional attraction to the idea of *being* a girl or woman. In any event, I felt comfortable with Alice immediately, despite the intervening years, and I remember holding her hand as her father drove my mother and me back to New York. But my strongest memory of that visit was a very brief exchange between us during the long conversation at her house. She mentioned having cried at someone's funeral, and I responded that for a girl that was all right. Then she said it was all right for a boy to cry, too. I doubt if I was convinced. My thinking was clearly restricted by gender stereotypes, and they would continue to limit me for decades to come.

For the first couple of years of high school, I actually had very little contact with girls. My role was that of a brain, so neither gender nor sexuality seemed that important, even though my environment constantly reinforced prevailing prejudices. Finally, around the same time as my visit to Alice, I asked one of the daughters of an old friend of my father's to my junior prom. Elizabeth and I already knew each other reasonably well from several gatherings of our families, and as two children of English professors we had more than a little in common. We were never really boyfriend and girlfriend; we were basically just kids who liked each other well enough and needed someone to go out with. We would continue to date until sometime after we both graduated, when she met somebody she liked better. There was already someone I liked better, but that is an understatement.

For Christmas vacation in my senior year, I went back to my old hometown to spend a week or so with the family of one of my old friends. I am not sure why I accepted the invitation, but perhaps I unconsciously hoped that it would turn out the way it did. It was the first time I had seen Paul since we moved. As he pointed out years later in a letter of reference he wrote for me, we had known each other literally all our lives: our mothers had been in the maternity ward together, and our families were close friends while we were growing up. He was going to a boarding school, so we were both actually going to be in town only for the vacation.

While with Paul, I briefly experienced a sort of classic 1950s teenage lifestyle very different from my own rather sheltered and atypical existence. In that town, as depicted later in the classic movie *American Graffiti,* adolescent life revolved around cars. The cooler the car, the cooler the kid. And Paul's car was cool. It was a red 1931 Ford Model A with a modern Chevy engine. Hopped-up classic oldies like that were a big deal back then, as was our friend's original-style Corvette. In a small town like that, those cars and many others were instantly recognized as their teen drivers cruised around in the evenings, stopping at the Dairy Queen to gather and drink milkshakes.

The first night I was there, we went to the annual Christmas dance at the college where my father had taught. The girl they had fixed me up with was cute but not my type. Not brainy enough. A day or two later I called Maggie. She said she had heard I was in town and wondered if I would call. So she had not forgotten me, either. Good sign. Then she asked me over and that evening Paul dropped me off at her house. We sat on their enclosed porch and started out by playing Scrabble. She beat me. No surprise there. As I said before, we had always been rivals. I cannot remember exactly what we did next but soon we were in each other's arms and it was like a lightning strike. The last few years disappeared in a flash and we were closer, more powerfully drawn together, than ever before. When Paul picked me up and asked what we had done, I said that we "made up for a whole lot of lost time."

There was no question in my mind that I was in love with Maggie. The only problem was that I already had a date for whatever Paul and I had planned for the following night. Maggie and I did not want anything or anyone to interfere with the few days we had to be together! Well fate, or the goddess, or whatever, must have taken our side, because the next morning the other girl called me at Paul's house and said she could not make it. My heart leapt at the same time that I told her how sorry I was. So of course I immediately called Maggie, and we were together again that evening.

We went to a party at the home of someone from her high school, and it was great fun. Maggie and I sat at the entrance to the recreation room, and greeted the steady stream of guests. I had known most of them before, but did not necessarily recognize them. As each person or couple approached, Maggie would tell me their names, I would greet them by name, and most of them would be amazed that I knew who they were.

Somehow they never caught on. In fact, one girl, the sister of a boy in my class, said, "I *know* you don't recognize *me.*" When I said, "Of course I do; you're Wendy Watkins," her stunned expression was priceless.

I went back home with joy in my heart. Being back together with my childhood sweetheart gave me a feeling of continuity and stability. We began writing each other faithfully, and when she was about to go to New York with her civics class, I asked her if I could see her there if I just "happened" to be in the city at the same time. Of course the teacher who was going with them said no, because if she let her do something like that on her own, she would have to let everyone, etcetera, etcetera.

That was no disaster, because we were both approaching graduation, which of course meant senior proms. Hers came first, and it was an amazing weekend. Her family seemed happy to have me there. The dance itself was great, and I really enjoyed seeing my old classmates. But I did have to be a little evasive with everyone who asked me where I was going to college. Only Maggie knew why.

What Maggie knew was that I wanted to become a priest and hoped to enter a Jesuit seminary in the fall. As much as we cared for each other, we thought we were approaching the end of the road. So I am going to put Maggie on hold for now, and show how my intention developed quite naturally from my high school experience.

The fundamental aspect of my school, at least for me, was that it was a Catholic school. That influenced everything about it. We had four years of religion class. The boarding students attended Mass every morning.

The whole class went on a retreat every year. A good example of the effect all of this had on us was what our class president said about the priest who directed our sophomore retreat. According to another student, he had said that the priest "did not scare us enough." That sums up one of the strongest messages I received for four years. Follow the rules of God and the Catholic Church or burn in hell forever. Fear as a major motive for how to live your life.

In fairness, the negative message was not the only one I received. I was also taught that being close to God was the most satisfying possible way to live, and that heaven was not just the way to avoid hell but also the highest possible state of existence. Here on earth, the closest thing to heaven was the priesthood. I definitely believed that priests were the holiest people on earth, although I may have thought my mother was a close second. Indeed, for me my mother was virtually the embodiment of Catholicism. I had little doubt that she was a saint.

She wanted me to be a priest. Not surprising, since she probably thought it was the best thing anyone could be. Nevertheless, I cannot help considering another possible reason. If she did wish that I were a girl, might she have thought that celibacy would be the next best thing? After all, a priest could be seen as being neither male nor female, at least in a sexual sense. I myself may have felt something similar. I recall that a retreat leader (probably the same one who did not scare us enough) told me I could make a profession to God that I intended to become a priest. And that same year I was quite disappointed to learn that the Catholic Church considered voluntary sterilization to be a form of self-mutilation and sinful. I had thought that perhaps I should be sterilized as a sort of active commitment to priestly celibacy. In my senior year, in addition to applying to colleges, I also applied to a Jesuit seminary. And that brings me back to Maggie and her prom.

At that time I fully intended to enter the seminary if I was accepted, and that was why I evaded questions about where I was going to college. But at some point between the prom itself and my trip home, I came to what may have been a life-changing realization. Being so close to Maggie, I suddenly knew that sometime I was going to want to marry someone. I would reconsider that before too long, but it did cause me to abandon the idea of the seminary. On the way back, I stopped in Washington to have dinner with my uncle's family and told them of my "change of heart," as one of my cousins put it. It was a good way to put it.

When I arrived home, there was no good way to put it to my mother. I assured her that it was not because I expected to marry Maggie, but simply because I would want to marry someone. She repeated the word "someone" in a tone and with an expression that seemed to indicate that she did not like the idea, no matter who it turned out to be. She made a slight effort to get me to reconsider, but quickly realized that I was not going to change my mind. When Maggie came up for my prom, the timing was unfortunate. Her plane arrived too late for her to get to the graduation and hear my valedictory speech. But I had missed hers, too. What bothered me more was that my father had to pick her up at the airport, so he missed it too. I am sure that was hard on him, especially since he wished I was taking Elizabeth to the prom.

The rest of the weekend was marvelous. Maggie was quite the sensation at the dance, because at that time a southern girl's idea of a prom dress was much more elegant than a northern girl's. The after-party that I remember best was at the home of a classmate. The property was so magnificent that when we arrived I thought we had driven up to some country club by mistake. Then we discovered that it was right on Lake Erie and had a sandy beach complete with indoor showers and locker rooms. It was the perfect place for a party, but of course my favorite part was Maggie. It was a wonderful night, and I think that some of my classmates who had thought of me as nothing but the class brain were surprised when they saw me with the right girl.

As for being the class brain, that image was overblown. The salutatorian was as good a student as I was and I edged him out by the slimmest of margins. Looking back, I wish they had made us co-valedictorians, the way they had done the previous year when faced with extremely close grade point averages. But I seem to have had a sort of mystique that set me apart. Perhaps I seemed more *intellectual.* In any event, my high school career ended on a very positive note. My college career would be a different story.

CHAPTER III

DOWNWARD SPIRAL

After my high school graduation, I must have looked as though I had it made. I was at the top of my class, had been accepted at an Ivy League college, had a girlfriend whom I loved, and had expectations of a bright academic future. Nor was that just how it seemed to others. I bought into that scenario myself. I decided to take summer courses at the local Jesuit college, and picked out two Latin courses that looked interesting. The only problem was that they were graduate courses. Undaunted, I went up to the professor and asked if I could enroll in them. He looked skeptical until I told him my score on the College Boards Latin achievement test. Then he said yes. I think I dropped one of the courses, but I did well in the other one. I had little doubt that I was ready for the Ivy League.

When I got to college, I quickly found that it was full of bright, confident kids who had been at the top of their classes in high school. That fact had both positive and negative effects on me. When I first met my roommate and a few other students in the dorm, I had the feeling that they were all brighter, more accomplished, or from more prominent families than I was. On the other hand, I soon discovered how cool it was that almost everyone I met shared my level of academic enthusiasm and was ready to engage in stimulating conversation.

I picked out some great-sounding courses to enroll in, one of which was a Shakespeare course taught by a leading Shakespeare scholar. I was able to take that course because I had advanced placement in English, and I was foolhardy enough to do so even though the famous professor announced on the first day that freshmen usually did not do well in it. An even bigger mistake was taking Russian. I had not shown much aptitude for modern languages in high school, and I was soon totally lost in that one. I managed to drop it and get into a Latin course that was relatively easy for me compared to the graduate course I had taken in the summer.

The fact that I was struggling academically was not the worst of it. That is not unusual for previously successful students in their first semester of college. My bigger problem was that I was floundering in a more personal sense. I remember that virtually every day I was trying to reinvent myself, trying out one idea after another of who and what I was. It was a bewildering experience, and before Christmas break I was in a total state of turmoil. What I longed for was some sense of peace. That was not a new sensation for me.

As a senior in high school I had a spiritual director, and I remember telling him that what I wanted was peace. He was not sure what kind of peace I meant, and I did not know how to explain it. Perhaps I simply meant freedom from turmoil. In any case, it was something I would search for, for decades. During that first college semester, the yearning took an extreme form. As a Catholic, I belonged to the college Newman Club, and

I started searching for a spiritual path to the peace I so urgently needed.

The quest led me to the books by Thomas Merton, the Trappist monk best known as the author of *The Seven Storey Mountain.* I had known of him in high school; in fact, I believe that he had been at Gethsemane Monastery when my class had gone there for our senior retreat. I had experienced a sense of peace there in the chapel during the wee hours of the morning, and now I felt that the monastic life was my true calling. Before leaving college for Christmas break, I told my roommate and another friend that I was "out of it," by which I think I meant that I was giving up on the competitive academic life in which we were engaged. I left for home with no intention of coming back.

When I arrived home, I must have looked like a mess. My parents' housekeeper said I looked like I had been on a binge, which I had definitely not. For the first few days I said nothing about college, but when I finally told them I was dropping out, Sam said they had suspected as much but were waiting to hear it from me. Then I dropped the other shoe.

When I said I wanted to become a monk, my father said that leaving college did not mean I had to go to such an extreme as that. Of course he was right, but I was too desperate to realize it. So I called someone at Gethsemane, and he told me that if I wanted to discuss a vocation, I should come down there for a retreat and talk to them there. I did not do that right away, and at some point around then we all went to Frank's wedding. I must have been very unsure about the monastery idea, because I got very drunk on champagne at the reception, and after sobering up I told my parents that "it was worth it." I think I meant that I was in such a state of emotional chaos that I welcomed the chance to just blot everything out for a few hours. As far as I can remember, that was the first of only three times in my life that I actually got sick from drinking.

Perhaps that debacle was what convinced me that I was not ready for monkhood. When I gave up that idea, my father thought I should go back to the Jesuit college where I had taken the Latin course. I think he figured that going to a Catholic college after my Catholic high school might make leaving an Ivy League college appear more comprehensible. I did enroll there, but I thought of it as only temporary. Actually, my semester there went well and I thought I should go back to college number one. I sometimes wonder how things would have worked out if I had stayed at college number two. But I have wondered that about a lot of things, and I have decided that I would not want to have done anything differently. Changing anything in the past would have completely unknown effects on the present. It is likely that I would not have my wife and children. I might not have reached my present religious understanding; might never have discovered my true gender identity; might not be writing this book. I am glad that all these things and many others have turned out the way they have.

I am also glad about most of my relationships with women. Those relationships have always been very special to me, and I think closeness to women has brought me closer to my own womanhood. I have already mentioned one of the most significant women in my life, Maggie. It was while attending college number two that

I saw her for the last time, although our relationship continued for a while. I visited her at her college for some big dance. It was a wonderful weekend. The dance itself was great fun. As I remember, a dance band from West Point supplied the music. Maggie showed me around the beautiful campus and introduced me to some of her friends and we had dinner at a very nice, very southern restaurant. One of the most significant events of the weekend occurred on Sunday morning.

As a Catholic, I lived under the requirement to attend Mass every Sunday and I asked Maggie to come with me. She was somewhat hesitant, but she did it. Then afterwards, as we were leaving the church, she asked, "Do you want to go to my church now? " I should have seen it coming but I did not. So I had about five seconds to make a crucial decision. Crucial because, just as the Catholic Church required Catholics to attend church, it also forbade us from attending any *other* church. I made the decision. "I'm not supposed to," I said. "But I will."

That was the first time I had ever deliberately defied the Church's rules. I was breaking the rules imposed upon me by others and doing what I thought was best for myself and for someone I loved. Interestingly enough, that weekend I also came up against another little rule, one less important but directly related to gender. At one point while we were walking along together, I took Maggie's hand but apparently did it the wrong way. When she adjusted the position of our hands so that mine was behind hers, I asked her what difference it made. "It makes a difference," she said. Did it? In a way, I guess it did. I think it must have been about who was leading whom. With the man's hand in the back, he would be leading her. The way it is supposed to be. Apparently, I was questioning the laws of nature as well as those of the Church.

How to hold hands was only one of a number of gender-related issues that came up around that time. I think that spring or summer may have been when Sam made several remarks that made an impression on me. One of these was an emphatic declaration that he would never wear a wedding ring. I will not speculate too much about the significance of only a wife wearing a wedding ring, but it certainly suggests a difference in the appropriate gender roles within a marriage. On another occasion, there was something on the radio about a male to female transsexual. Sam said that "he" would never be a woman. When I challenged that, he said something like, "Well, he'll never be able to have children." Was he implying that having children is part of the definition of a woman? Or at least a necessary part of a woman's role in life?

Sam's disapproval of transsexual women apparently extended to other women who challenged generally accepted gender roles. I remember telling him, probably with some enthusiasm, about two feminists I had heard on the radio. He promptly asserted that they did not want to be women. Another time, he said he thought that all women (or perhaps he did not quite say "all") wanted to be married. I questioned that, and he said I was not very romantic. But then my father said he thought it actually *was* a rather romantic idea that a woman would want to be independent and live her own way. Interesting, considering that he himself could be somewhat sexist. One time, during a discussion about politics, he said that most women just vote the same way as their husbands. Maybe back then, but you certainly could not prove it by the "gender gap" that is so common in elections these days.

Traditional gender roles were not the only values I was challenging that summer. It was also a pivotal point in my religious life. Let me set the context. I was taking a couple of courses at college number two, the Jesuit college while waiting to hear whether I would be readmitted to college number one, the Ivy League college. One of the courses I was taking was metaphysics, and the professor was a feisty Jesuit with whom I enjoyed arguing. But during one exchange, he suddenly said, "You don't talk like a Catholic." As I pondered that remark later on, it occurred to me that if I did not sound like a Catholic, maybe it was because I no longer really *was* a Catholic. That thought made me do some literal soul-searching.

The search led me to the somewhat surprising conclusion that I had somehow lost my faith. It was not that I thought I had proven Catholic teachings to be invalid. It was just that for some unclear reason I no longer believed. Perhaps prophetically, I was giving up what I had thought was my religious identity to seek my true self.

As a result, I made a couple of immediate changes. One was mostly symbolic and was probably intended as a statement to myself that I truly was done listening to the Catholic Church. It consisted of eating a hamburger on Friday. In case some of my readers do not already know this, back then the Church forbade Catholics from eating meat on Friday. That fact was so well known that

some people almost seemed to think it was the main difference between Catholics and Protestants! A more
meaningful change was that I stopped going to Mass on
Sunday. This was so significant, indeed, that for a while
I actually dressed up as though for church but then went
someplace else, so that my devoutly Catholic mother
would not know.

Of course the behavioral changes were not as important in my life as the changes in how I thought and felt.
On one hand, I had pulled he rug out from under
myself. All the firm beliefs that had anchored me were
gone, and I felt adrift in a vast sea without a compass.
But the flip side was that my thoughts were no longer
constrained by so many prior assumptions. I was now
free to travel wherever in the cosmos my mind and heart
might lead me. And the beginning of the trip was to go
from a college steeped in Catholicism back to what I
considered to be a citadel of academic knowledge and
intellectual exploration.

But first, as though losing my faith was not enough
for one summer, I also had a totally unexpected change
in my affections. Despite how close Maggie and I were
emotionally, geographically we were so far apart that we
both dated other people at home. Since I was no longer
seeing Elizabeth, I called up Joanie. She was the former
girlfriend of my best friend in high school, and I had
always liked her. I asked her out and she said yes and
before we knew what was happening lightning struck.
One night we were at a drive-in movie and I said her
name, and she said, "Did you call?" I asked, "If I called,
would you come?" She replied, "I'm yours." And so it
was, for the next year and a half. I could hardly believe

that anyone could replace Maggie, but the mutual mag-
netism was so strong that there was no turning back.

I got the approval to return to college number one,
and although it meant starting out as a freshman all over
again, I was ready and willing. At first I was in a single
room because the student who was supposed to room
with me had a change in plans. I got off to a good start
meeting other people in my dorm, though. I think I was
less intimidated by them than I had been the year before.
I was now, for better or for worse, an old hand at being
an Ivy League freshman. At this point, I felt that I really
belonged there. Joanie and I were exchanging letters regularly, and I managed to take care of the difficult task of
writing a good-bye letter to Maggie. It was, after all, the
end of a very long, close, and caring relationship. She
replied with a touching letter expressing both disap-
pointment and acceptance of the situation. I was moving
on with my life, and I knew that she would move on
with hers.

One day a student I had never seen before showed
up at my door and handed me a note from some dean.
It basically just said that the bearer thereof was looking
for a roommate and asked me to consider letting him
room with me. I had probably always figured that someone would be moved in sooner or later, and my response
was something along the lines of "yeah, sure." He
thought we should get to know each other first and pro-
ceeded to tell me the story of how his former roommate
had turned his alarm clock off, making him late for a
test or paper deadline or whatever. In light of that, I
could understand why he wanted to check me out before
moving in. I guess I met his criteria for a non-risky

roommate, and I had no problem with him, so he moved in. We never really became friends, but for the most part we coexisted fairly peacefully except for a couple of arguments about relatively unimportant things. The bottom line was probably that neither one of us had much in the way of social graces. Even so, we both managed to fit in reasonably well with separate and very different groups of students.

For me, the key was becoming friends with Dale, who lived on the floor above me with two or three other guys. In some ways, we were quite different. I was a preppie and he had gone to public schools in upstate New York. My father was a college professor and his worked for the railroad. He had been senior class president and was something of a natural athlete. I had been neither. Perhaps the most obvious similarity was that we were both taking classical Greek. But he did all right in it and I squeaked by with the worst grade I had ever had in anything. Still, there was definitely something that drew us together. In fact I think he was the first of only two real male friends I ever had in college.

Dale and I often hung out with one of his roommates, and both of them came to my aid in the wake of my disastrous Greek final exam. Knowing how badly I had done, I bought a pint of scotch and went back to the dorm to drown out the memory. I remember sitting on the bottom step of the staircase from my floor to Dale's, getting progressively sloshed. One of the proctors asked Dale about the exam and he said I was forgetting it. After I finished off the bottle, he and his roommate took me outside to walk it off and when we got back I went to bed. The next morning I woke up surprisingly clearheaded, and got to work studying for the rest of my exams (Greek having been the first). I cannot really recommend that method of dealing with an academic setback, but it worked that time.

All in all, that was a good year. Despite the Greek fiasco, I had pretty good grades and really enjoyed some of my courses. One of them was in political science and prompted me to declare that as my major. The course also made it clear what my academic strength was. A student in the room next to mine was also taking it, and I could tell that he knew more going into the final exam than I did. But I did at least as well as he did. It was an essay exam, and apparently I could express whatever amount I did know more effectively than he could. Verbal expression was definitely my strong suit.

Joanie and I kept in touch by letters and spent lots of time together on vacations. On New Year's Eve, we went to one of the three or four old-fashioned ballrooms that still existed in our city. Dancing was always one of our favorite things to do together, and even now, at my ripe old age, people often seem surprised at how energetic I can get on a dance floor. Christmas vacation that year was also memorable for me because of the driving conditions. I had a car and drove home with three others in very nasty weather.

The school year ended and I went home for the summer feeling pretty good about myself. It looked as though I was back on track. I wanted to do some kind of work over the summer, and decided to look for a volunteer job. My theory was that I could find something more interesting that way than with a paying job. I found some sort of research job at a hospital and was even written up in a newspaper as an example of a young person doing volunteer work. But for some reason, I quit shortly after the article was published. Looking back, I see that as just one event in a long-lasting pattern of giving up on something instead of carrying it on to fruition. In hindsight, I have to think that nothing ever seemed like a good fit for me because the person I was trying to be never fit the person I really was.

I believe that my relationship with Joanie was also ceasing to be as good a fit as it had seemed. We saw each other several times a week and continued to have a lot of good times, but it seemed that we were also arguing more and that I increasingly felt that I had to agree with her and do things her way in order to keep peace. Difficulty in being assertive without being too aggressive is another problem that followed me through the years. Decades later, my therapist told me that I was as full of stereotypes as anybody. I am sure that those stereotypes included the idea that men were supposed to be assertive, even aggressive, while women were supposed to be compliant. So what was *I* supposed to be?

One nice thing that happened during the summer was that Dale, who was going to be my roommate for the coming year, visited me at home. I took him to meet Joanie and then Carl, who used to date her, both on the same day. That seemed a little awkward to me, but it went smoothly, and Dale appeared to like both of them. The next time I saw him was at the end of the summer, when I picked him up on the way back to school. We went out with his parents for dinner, and then he and I went to a movie at a local art house. In the morning we headed off to school. It all felt good, as though I was finally experiencing college life the way it was supposed to be. It turned out to be the calm before the storm.

At first, everything seemed all right. We moved into our new dorm and connected with Dale's former roommates, who were rooming together in that same dorm. I made a deal with a nearby homeowner to park my car in his yard, which I had been told I should do. Dale and one of the former roommates and I continued to hang around together, and after dinner we would go to the common room, where I would write a letter to Joanie while they played chess. That may have fueled a feeling that I had even the year before: I felt like an interloper, as though I had managed to insert myself into a friendship where I did not really belong. It seemed that the real friendship was between the two of them and that I once again did not fit in.

At the same time, I was dealing with some other disturbing thoughts and events. In my political science seminar, we were talking about American policy toward the Soviet Union. I proposed that, since we were still ahead in the arms race, we should attack them before they caught up. The idea understandably alarmed some of the other students, but the seminar leader suggested that I develop it in my first paper.

Ironically, I made my hawkish statement just before the Cuban missile crisis. When the Soviet Union deployed missiles in Cuba, just ninety miles from our shores, President Kennedy basically told them that if they did not take them out, we would take them out. Or at least that was how it appeared at the time. For almost a week, everyone held his breath wondering whether World War III was about to start. Quite shaken,

I roamed around the dorm that evening looking for my seminar leader. I did not find him, but I did run into one of the other members of the seminar, who said something like, "It feels different now that it may happen, doesn't it?" I don't think it changed my mind, but it certainly was frightening.

The Soviets backed down, the missiles went away, and Kennedy was a hero. (It was not yet known that he had secretly agreed to remove American missiles from Turkey.) But I still had a lot of anxiety. I did not have the optimism I had had the previous year. At some point, perhaps before the missile scare, I contacted my uncle who was a doctor, and asked him to help me find a psychiatrist. He gave me a name and I made a call, but the psychiatrist did not get back to me for a few weeks. By then I was feeling as though I might not make it through the semester. I made an appointment and went to see him. At the end of the session, he said I was not well and that it might not be a bad idea if I dropped out again. Hearing it hurt, but I was not really surprised.

I contacted my parents, who were already thinking about getting a second residence somewhere in the Southwest. It was agreed that I would go out there with them. I dropped out of college number one for the second time and off we went. The first order of business was to find a house. We looked at several and ended up renting a nice but unremarkable house in Scottsdale, Arizona. Its most distinctive feature was a front yard full of grapefruit trees.

After we moved in, I had to confront an issue I had been trying to ignore for about three weeks. What about Joanie? Was our relationship going to survive? I finally faced the music and called her up. I knew I was in trouble when her sister answered and I heard her ask Joanie if she wanted to talk to me. A month before, there would have been no doubt that she would want to. I heard her say yes and she got on the phone, but the conversation was a disaster. She was very hurt by the way I had just disappeared and made such an important decision without even talking to her about it. And she had clearly dealt with the situation by relegating our relationship to the past. It was over. I was devastated. After hanging up I broke into tears.

For the first time in almost four years, I was without a girlfriend. That would be one of the hardest things about my Arizona period. Girls had been my lifeline. Perhaps my unconscious need to be a girl expressed itself as a need to be very close to a girl. Years later, it would seem clear to me that my real desire was always to be a girl who liked girls.

I had only a couple of dates during that period, and no second dates. For the first few months, I also had no male friends and felt quite lonely and isolated. I spent quite a lot of time shopping for one thing or another, partly to have sales people to talk to. I met a few people that way with whom I could probably have become friends, but something held me back. I was probably afraid of rejection. Two guys who worked in an audio store actually invited me to come back some time just to visit. But even though I felt that we had something in common, I never went back.

I did meet a couple of people through one of my old hobbies. I still had the ham radio license I got while in high school, so I answered a classified ad for some used equipment and went on the air. Two of the hams I contacted invited me over to see their stations; I went but made no attempt to form ongoing relationships with them. To increase my knowledge of electronics, I considered enrolling in a local trade school, but I never did. The reason I gave myself was that I could not figure out where I could eat lunch while going there! Maybe it never occurred to me to call the admissions person and ask what other students did about lunch. Or maybe I just could not miss the chance to flush one more opportunity down the drain.

Before we had been in Arizona very long, my father found a psychiatrist for me and made an appointment. I missed the first appointment, so he made another. He told me the doctor had said that if I missed again he would not give me any more appointments. I did go and continued seeing him as long as I was there. I cannot say the experience was extremely helpful, but a couple of significant things did happen. I think he was the first person I ever told that I was really a woman and not a man. He said, "You *look* like a man." I replied that I was a man physically, but felt hat I was a woman psychologically. Then he asked if I thought there was a psychological difference between men and women. I assume that I said "yes," but he never pursued it at all. So this was also my first experience of the mental health community's almost total lack of understanding about what would turn out to be my core psychological issue.

Meanwhile, I was still trying to figure out what to do with myself. When the doctor said there were two basic possibilities, I said that I thought so too, and that they were doing everything or doing nothing. He probably meant going back to college or getting a job, but my response illustrates the extremist way I was thinking. All or nothing. Either my father or I got the idea of opening a bookstore, which he and Frank had once done. We leased a store and spent some time deciding what inventory we needed, but of course I backed out.

When summer came, I did go back to college, at the nearby state university. I took two courses and did very well. In general, summer courses went better for me than the regular school year. It seemed that I could maintain focus better with a concentrated effort for five or six weeks than when I had to divide my attention among several courses and over a longer period of time. When I finally got a degree, a substantial number of my credits were from summer courses.

Although the summer was going well academically, some other things I was involved in did not go so smoothly. I did, however, finally make a friend. He was Barry, the director of the Baptist Student Union. It would turn out that during my years of agnosticism I nevertheless tended to hang around religion in one way or another. I do not remember what drew me to the Baptist group, but I found it to be a friendly bunch and Barry and I hit it off especially well. The only problem was that I was completely faking the religious part of it, pretending to be a believer. The charade made me uncomfortable, and I finally admitted what was going on. Barry and I, however, remained friends.

Something else I became involved in while going to that university was conservative politics. I was, after all, in the state of Barry Goldwater, the Republican Senator who was considered the standard bearer of the conservative movement (and who would get slaughtered when he ran for President a couple of years later). I found my way easily into conservative circles. I joined Young Americans for Freedom (YAF) and the ultra-conservative John Birch Society. We all shared an exciting feeling that we were a special group of enlightened patriots who were fighting to save America from the international communist conspiracy and its unwitting liberal lackeys. This was my first foray into the world of political extremism that would carry me into the far right, the far left, and even anarchism. But my search for political solutions to the world's problems would be interrupted by the search for a solution to my own problems.

As the summer ended and the fall semester began, I was beginning to feel the way I had felt during my final months at college number one. Through the summer, I had managed to maintain a sort of precarious balance among the emotional forces that were pulling me in all directions. But now, any such balance was giving way to inner turmoil that I could not control. I dropped out of college mid-term for the third time, and this time I was out of options. My parents and I came to an agreement that it was time for me to go someplace where a team of experts might be able to figure out what had been disrupting my life for the last three years. The result was that before long we would be driving up to one of the most respected mental hospitals in the country.

CHAPTER IV

THE HOSPITAL

When we arrived at the hospital, the sight that greeted us was nothing like the grim, foreboding appearance of the mental hospitals we have all seen in movies. Nor was the admission process particularly intimidating. I had a positive attitude and expected great benefits. I met my roommate and he seemed like a nice guy, although he was only seventeen and I was twenty-one. The first night I also met someone I had a lot in common with. We were the same age and we had both been attending Ivy League colleges. We also both liked folk music (though it would have been hard not to if you were a college student at that time). We spent part of the evening listening to it. It was nice to connect with someone so quickly, but I was fairly nervous and spent much of the time pacing back and forth in the common room where the music was playing.

It was probably the next day that I first met my house doctor, Dr. Kean. The system there was that everyone had a house doctor right from the start and would probably get a therapist later on. The house doctor would come to see you every day and was pretty much in charge of your life. It helped if you liked him or her, and I did. In fact, I told another patient that I regarded Dr. Kean as my mentor.

One of the first things Dr. Kean did was set up a daily schedule for me. Great emphasis was placed on structure in a patient's life, especially in the early stages of treatment. There was a whole range of activities available. One of mine was a ham radio class, and that boosted my confidence, since I was already licensed. I am not sure which other ones I was in at the beginning, but at one point or another I did ceramics, jewelry making, woodworking, and even gardening.

I think one of the purposes of all these programs, besides keeping us busy, was to give people who had pretty well messed up their lives the experience of doing something successfully. It served that purpose for me, anyway. The programs were by no means just busywork. I learned a lot and completed some fairly impressive projects. My biggest achievement was building all the components of a high-quality stereo system from kits. I had worked on various electronics projects in high school and even junior high, but with the big ones I had given up on more than I had completed. To make this accomplishment even more satisfying, I also built speaker baffles and a cabinet for the equipment.

Not everything I tried worked out that well. My first effort in woodworking was turning a very nice-looking bowl on a lathe. I had turned a much less ambitious one in the eighth grade and had wanted to use a lathe again ever since. But when I was almost finished on the one at the hospital, I suddenly cut myself. Surprisingly, what actually cut me was not the chisel but the thin edge of the bowl itself. The wound was minor, but it did put an end to my use of power tools in the woodshop. When I talked to Dr. Kean about it, I admitted that at times I had felt like deliberately shoving the chisel into the bowl to destroy it. I was not attempting that when I hurt myself, but I have to wonder whether I had subconsciously turned my anger or whatever it was onto myself instead of the bowl. I do not remember what Dr. Kean said about it.

Not all of the activities available for patients involved making things. There were also many that helped us learn to work together and gave us opportunities to develop leadership skills. I had always liked to run things, and I lost no time in attempting to run some of the patient activities. My first chance was the weekly meeting in our section of the hospital. I had also always had some instinct for politics, so when the current floor leader stepped down, I asked him for his support if I ran for the office. He said that some people did not like me, but I knew I did not need all the votes, and I talked him into supporting me anyway.

I was elected, and I suppose I did the job reasonably well, but I got caught in a power struggle between two older patients. They both tried to influence me to side with them, and by the end of my term I was worried that I might lose the next election. But Dr. Kean said that winning or not was less important than whether I should stay in such an uncomfortable position. I guess he convinced me, because I did not even run that time. Later on, however, I did have other leadership opportunities.

For a while I chaired the committee on evening activities, which planned dances and other events. Unfortunately, my only clear memory of that is an argument with another patient about what music should be played at a dance. Actually, I must have shown some sort of aptitude, because one evening after my term had ended, a committee member rushed up to me and asked me to go downstairs and introduce some performance that I had no interest in. I did, and then went back upstairs.

The most important committee for patient involvement was the patient council. I was secretary of that for a while, and at some point after I became a day patient, the social worker in charge of it asked me to be chairperson. By then, however, I was going to the local college and had a conflict with a course I was taking. It was annoying that when I finally had a chance at the top spot, I had to turn it down. But being secretary may have been the best position for me anyway, since writing was my best strength. That strength also got me onto several other projects. At one point I was in a group formed to rewrite a patient handbook, which was a good experience in collaboration. I was also on the staff of our literary magazine, although I do not think I contributed much to that effort. Even worse, I wrote a very critical evaluation of one submission and then discovered that its author was our editor and also that I had completely missed the point. My stint as editor of the patient newsletter went better. Even so, I told Dr. Kean that it made me feel like a prostitute. I am not sure what I meant, except that something about using my writing ability must have made me uncomfortable. He said he wanted me to continue anyway.

A good many years later, during a conversation with some friends, someone mentioned a group of mental patients in New York who were fighting to increase the rights of mental patients. A woman whose husband was a friend of mine, and whom I liked and respected in her own right, suddenly said that the idea of mental patients trying to organize anything seemed amusing. I somehow suppressed the urge to tell her how many of them I had worked with in sundry organizations and how many projects we had planned and carried out successfully. That part of my personal history was still unknown to almost everyone I was involved with at that time, and I was not going to let it out of the bag, despite how much I hated such extreme misrepresentations of people struggling with mental illness. Nor could I blame the woman for promulgating the stereotypes. She was only reflecting the pervasive prejudices of our society, at least at that time.

So far, I have been writing primarily about the good aspects of being at the hospital. But I do not want to give the impression that it was all smooth sailing. It was not. Much of the time I felt like hell. There was an axiom that you have to get worse before you can get better. That certainly describes my experience there. I think the idea was that all of us had built up various coping mechanisms and defense strategies so as to keep functioning despite having serious psychological problems. But before those problems can be treated, they must be laid bare by removing the defenses that have been maintained for a long time.

I have said that the hospital did not look like fictional representations of mental hospitals. The patients were nothing like most representations, either. No one thought he was Franklin Roosevelt or Jesus or the Queen of England. Few ever seemed hysterical. I heard very little screaming and saw hardly any violent behavior. Most of the patients would not have seemed

crazy or even especially unusual if you met them somewhere else. They had varied backgrounds, though in
most cases their families were well enough off to be able
to afford the place. For some of them, that would be an
understatement. I knew several whose last names were
the names of major corporations, and not by coincidence. One patient was the sister of a senator, and
another was the daughter of a governor. One was the
daughter of a famous musician, and another was the son
of a movie star. One patient was a psychiatrist. It is my
strict policy never to reveal the name of anyone I knew
there.

Of course, most of us were not from famous families. Most were just people who, because of one psychological problem or another, had lost the ability to
function in a constructive way. One effect of being there
was that it gave us all experience and guidance in inter-
acting with other people. This had been a deficiency for
many of us, definitely including myself. I spent countless
hours talking with other patients about almost anything
you could think of, and many were bright, well educated, and interesting. Not that we did not sometimes
lose control and do or say something totally unacceptable. Case in point: one time I was in the dining room
at a table with my best friend there and a generally pleasant young woman. She said something I did not like and
I suddenly called her a bitch, in a voice loud enough to
be heard throughout the room. My friend promptly
defused the situation by shepherding me out of the
room, into the elevator, and up to our floor. He told me
that she was being exactly what I said, but that you cannot say it.

And that introduces Tom. I do not remember when or how I met him, but we soon became fast friends. We had intellectual interests in common and were just generally comfortable with one another. I assume that he was there because of attempting suicide. His wrist was still badly scarred from the attempt, and he had no use of that hand. I felt especially bad about that because he had been a good pianist and was now reduced to one-handed piano practice. But before leaving the hospital, he had an operation that gave him back much of the use of the hand, and I think he was able to play again.

One day I walked into the lounge, and Tom was there, and he asked me to sit down so we could have a "tête-à-tête." I said, "Sounds sexy," and he responded, "You ask for what most people try to avoid." I asked what he meant and he said I knew. I did. At that time I was thinking that I might be homosexual. I have since learned that such thoughts are not uncommon for people who have not yet found their true gender identity.

I discussed those feelings with both Dr. Kean and my therapist, Dr. White. Neither of them seemed to take it very seriously. They apparently defined sexual orientation as behavior, not feelings or attraction. And since homosexuality was still considered a mental illness, the bias was toward my not being gay. When I told Dr. Kean that I might be a latent homosexual, he said I could just as well consider myself a latent heterosexual. Dr. White said that I only talked about it when I wanted to "drive people away." They both turned out to be right that I was not a gay man, but it never occurred to either them or me that I might be a gay *woman*. What if they had tried to get me to talk more about those feelings? Could it have led to some insight into my true sexuality and my true gender identity? Unfortunately, at the time it was assumed that gender depends on anatomy, rather than feelings. Even the doctors at what was considered a state-of-the-art mental hospital had virtually no understanding of gender as the word is used today. I shudder when I remember that they had a group of female patients who were supposed to get together to sew and do other "womanly" things, apparently to become more like what the overwhelmingly male psychiatric profession thought women should be.

As I said, much of the time I felt like hell. I remember clearly that for a long time my greatest wish was to reach a point where the way I felt was a way I could stand feeling for the rest of my life. That time did come. At some point I realized that I felt decent enough to imagine going on like that. The way the hospital and hospital life were organized seemed designed to promote and reinforce a sense of progress. When I got there, everyone lived in the same building, but it was divided into three units. One unit was for patients who needed the closest supervision, and I believe it was used for the relatively few who had displayed violent behavior. I was never there.

The largest unit, which most people entered upon arrival, was sort of the core of the hospital. That was where we stayed while coming to understand our primary problems and beginning to learn what could be done about them. The first order of business after arrival was a battery of psychological and even neurological tests. I was told that I did well enough on the intelligence-based tests but not so well on the ones designed to assess physical performance. As a result, I was examined by a neurologist, but he did not find anything significant. Then I had to face what was expected to be a long road to mental health. It was the sixties, when really long-term treatment was in style.

The third unit was for patients who were doing quite well and approaching the point when they would be ready to move out and become day patients. The only remaining step was outpatient, which meant living on one's own and coming to the hospital only for therapy appointments and perhaps a few activities. That was the last of a sequence of steps that provided gradual increases of freedom. The first few steps were so restrictive that I experienced a long and very unpleasant feeling of confinement. I think that feeling was probably even more acute for many of the other patients, since I was there voluntarily, rather than having been committed.

When I first arrived, I had to turn over all money and identification. That in itself would have slowed down the process of leaving, even though I had the legal right to do so. Then I was assigned to "group" status, which meant I could not go anywhere, even downstairs to the dining room, except as part of a group escorted by a staff member. Not a pleasant situation. Next came permission to go to scheduled activities on one's own. After that came the coveted "grounds" status, when you could finally go anywhere on the hospital campus. And then you could start asking your doctor to let you go off grounds for a specific purpose. As simple as just walking around the grounds must sound, when I got to that point I must have been afraid of even that: I had a dream about doing it naked. That is how Dr. Kean interpreted it, and now that seems pretty obvious. Even when I became comfortable with that status, I was very nervous about breaking the rules even slightly. One day my friend Tom asked me if I wanted to go over to a small zoo that was right across the street. I went, but felt guilty. When I told Dr. Kean, he seemed pretty unconcerned and just said that I really should stay on the grounds.

The way I felt at the zoo that day is an example of the way I felt for much of my life. Out of place. One time Dr. Kean asked me about that. I had just told him that the reason I was usually late for things was that it is almost impossible to be exactly on time, and I was afraid of being early. He asked if being early would make me feel out of place, and I said yes. I always thought I needed an excuse for being wherever I was, that no one would want me around unless I had a specific reason. That, I suppose, no one would want me around just as myself. Ultimately, I now have to think, it was because I could not know what I would fit into until I knew what the "I" was. Two common expressions come to mind. One is that someone feels like "a square peg in a round hole. " Not knowing *which* kind of peg I was, how could I know which kind of hole I belonged in? The other expression is that someone is "comfortable in his own skin." For most of my life, my female self was very literally not comfortable in my male skin.

I continued, however, to find some comfort with women. (Perhaps it was a sense of *belonging*.) Not long after arriving at the hospital, I started spending a lot of time with a woman I shall call Margaret. Eventually, I thought of her as something of a flake, but I think that at first I was attracted by her intensity. And, as they say, any port in a storm. As it turned out, I would be only one of a whole series of (supposed) men with whom she had close relationships until she switched to another one. I saw a miniature example of that even while I seemed to be her favorite. One evening (Christmas or New Year's or some special time like that), we had planned to eat dinner together. But when I got to the dining room, she was already at a table with another guy. Hurt, resentful, and even a bit disoriented, I joined a man and woman who were friends of mine. After a while, Margaret came over and said, "Now you know why I don't make dates." Except, of course, she had.

I am fuzzy on the chronology, but when the other woman at the table had just come to the hospital, I had a crush on her. Dr. Kean was her doctor too, and when he asked her if she had made any friends there, she said only me. Then he asked me what I had in common with her, and I said we were both interested in theater and things like that. But I think it was mainly just that I was attracted to her and she needed someone to latch onto in her early weeks there. Oh yes, and she was a redhead. But before long, she lost interest in me and attached herself to someone older and definitely more charming. I do not remember being interested in any other women while we were both in the hospital. But there would be someone while *I* was still in the hospital.

At some point I began going out to the movies with several other people, mostly women, if I remember correctly. One of them was a girl I had not really known while she was in the hospital, and now she was a day patient living with a local family. We clearly liked each other, and after a while we began sitting together rather than with the others. We also started sometimes eating lunch together at the college that we were both attending. At some point Dr. Kean asked me if those evenings were really dates for Meghan Hope and me. I said no, partly because neither of us had expressed looking at them that way, but also because I was afraid that he would not approve. In general, dating other patients was discouraged.

But eventually my feelings for Meghan Hope built up to the point that I had to risk his disapproval and, more importantly, the possibility that she did not feel the same way. It was during one of our lunches at the college snack bar that I took the plunge and told her how I felt. She said she did too, and suddenly I heard some guardian angels somewhere singing the "Hallelujah Chorus." We made a real date, just for us, and then of course I had to tell Dr. Kean. I was pretty apprehensive, but he had no problem with it and all systems were go.

We were young and in love. A couple of years before, we had both hit bottom, but now the present was looking up and the future was looking possible. We still went to movies on Saturday nights, now clearly as a couple. Sometimes we went to a foreign film series organized by the doctors at the hospital and sometimes to a little art theater. Once when we came out of that one with a mutual friend, we found that phone service was out and we had no way to call a cab.

After spending a few minutes wondering what to do, I got the idea of going into a liquor store to see if I could find somebody who would take us back into the part of town that still had phone service. I offered a man there five bucks, which was worth a lot more forty-plus years ago. It worked beautifully, and a day or two later

Meghan Hope told me that the other woman with us had been very impressed by the way I handled the situation. *Very* much later, my first wife said that I handled emergencies well. I just wish I could have handled things better the rest of the time.

One of the things I really liked during our relationship was the chance to meet each other's parents. We did not actually do a lot with hers, though we did spend some time with her mother. I never really saw much of her father, and I am sorry about that because I think I would have liked him. We seemed to do a little more with my parents when they visited. I remember one time when we drove with them to another town that my father wanted to see for some reason. Another time they took us to a very good restaurant in the nearest big city. My parents seemed to like Meghan Hope.

The two of us did some really nice things together. One time we went to that same restaurant that we had been to with my parents, and another time we went somewhere else in that city with another couple for New Year's Eve. We went to a few Grand Ole Opry shows in a nearby venue, and I still get a kick out of having seen and heard the likes of Roy Acuff, Roger Miller, and Ernest Tubb, the Texas Troubadour. Some of our best times were while I was still in the hospital but living in North Village, a group of three buildings that was the new residence for patients who were approaching the point of moving out and becoming day patients. Two attractive modern buildings housed patients in a style more like apartment living, in contrast with the more institution-like main building. There was no nurse's station, only a desk for a single nurse. We moved freely in and out on our own schedules, and most of us were either working or in school.

Meghan Hope routinely met me there, and we were well known as a couple. When my favorite roommate moved in, he was surprised to see the large photograph of her on my desk, because "patients aren't supposed to date patients." We were an exception. Our doctors apparently thought our relationship had a positive effect for both of us, perhaps partly because we accepted certain rules. I especially remember one summer when I would come back after an evening with Meghan Hope and sit around an outdoor table with a group that I called "the round table club." The only hint that I might not be doing quite as well as I thought was that a doctor who was substituting for Dr. Kean said that except for Meghan Hope my life seemed pretty empty.

My next move was into the home of a family who were in a program developed as an intermediate step between being in the hospital and living on one's own. The family I lived with was very nice, although there was a pretty great cultural difference. My father's predictably aristocratic summary was that they were "common." Things continued to go well for a while, but then I became generally dissatisfied, dropped out of some courses, and eventually just left town without telling anyone, even Meghan Hope. I know that hurt her. After a number of phone calls, I returned with the understanding that I would now have an apartment of my own. When I got back, Dr. Kean let me basically structure my life as I wanted. I moved into a furnished apartment in a hotel, and again things seemed to go well for a while. But soon my relationship with Meghan Hope started to fall apart. Or, to be honest, *I* started to fall apart.

Meghan Hope had always been ahead of me in treatment, and now I seemed to be slipping backwards while she was getting healthier. My mind was flying off in all directions. I remember her saying that in a single day I had mentioned six different professions I was thinking of going into, including both priest and pornographer! I also did a couple of things that really hurt her and that I deeply regret. When she finally ended our relationship, I think she was doing the only thing she could do.

The breakup hit me very hard. In an attempt to dull the pain, I soon began to date another girl I had known for a while. She was another redhead named Meghan, and even she remarked that it was not a very hard transition for me. Actually, it was an impossible transition, and the main thing I remember doing with her was drinking together. I think a lot of people try to substitute alcohol for love, but of course it never works, because there is no substitute for love. My life became increasingly disorganized. When a friend finally got his boss to offer me a job at the store where he worked, I turned it down because I had started to volunteer at a nonprofit organization. That did not last long, and after that I looked into buying or starting a bookstore. Of course I dropped that idea too. Feeling once again that I had no options, I retreated back into the hospital. But within two months, I realized that I did not belong there any longer. I left against medical advice, but by that time I had a clear goal: to finish college in two more semesters.

Somehow I held onto that goal, and it kept me focused. I did not let anything distract me from achieving it. I deliberately did not contact the second Meghan, and I had only a few dates, mostly with different women. I did switch my politics again, this time from far right to far left, under the influence of one of the women. As a result, I switched from smoking hand-carved Danish pipes and imported tobacco to cheap pipes and a brand of tobacco named Union Leader. I also gave up my luxury car in favor of a small and relatively cheap one that I guess I thought was more working-class. I was still drinking, but managed to keep it under enough control so that it did not interfere with my determination to get my college degree.

Graduation finally came. It was one of the worst days of my life. During the ceremony, my seat was directly behind Meghan Hope's, and I saw for the first time that she was wearing an engagement ring. To make matters even worse, when we came out of the auditorium I saw her with her parents and fiancé. I had not invited anyone, not even my parents, so I had no one to eat dinner with. I was going to a party given by the girl I had most recently dated a couple of times, and that should have helped, but I went to it with an empty stomach and drank too much and got sick all over the patio.

As bad as that was, the next day I did something that went really well. I called Meghan Hope. As soon as she heard my voice, she started to say that she had nothing to say to me, but I assured her that I was not going to make a scene, and that I was calling to congratulate her on both graduating *summa cum laude* and her engagement. I added that I realized she might doubt my sincerity, but she assured me that she did not. That meant a lot to me. We then talked for a few minutes and parted on a positive note. If I had not made that call, I do not think we could have ever re-established contact.

My business in that town was finished. I had applied to three graduate schools, been accepted at two, and decided to return to college number two, the Jesuit college I had attended before. Although my undergraduate major had been English, I had taken a lot of history courses, and that was what I was going to pursue in graduate school. New major, new life. I pointed my car toward home, ready to start over.

CHAPTER V

STARTING OVER

The drive home was interesting. I had very much the feeling that I was leaving one thing behind and going toward something new. On the way I stopped to see something that related to my interest in history: a historical society where I had a fruitful discussion with the director. His views and experience were of special interest to me because at that point it was a career that I thought I might want for myself. It also seemed especially relevant, since the academic requirement was a master's degree in history and that was exactly what I was about to start working on.

When I arrived home after the longest and most tiring road trip I had yet taken, I checked into a motel where I believe I stayed until I found an apartment. I may have spent part of that time at my parents' home, but I know it was important to me to remain as independent of them as I had been before returning. As a matter of fact, when I had decided to come back for graduate school, I told them that I would have my own apartment. A few years later, indeed, I learned that my father had not even liked the idea of my return to that city. I found that out from a former teacher who had suggested that I do my graduate work there. He had made the suggestion in my parents' living room one time when I was visiting them before returning, and he told me that my father had later said he did not appreciate his getting me to come back. So that describes what sort of family reunion it was at first.

I found an apartment that I liked a lot, and before school started I looked around for various radical political groups in the area. I found a couple, including one on the campus of another local university. It may or may not have been a branch of the Students for a Democratic Society, but I clearly remember going to one of their meetings and talking to someone who had just received his SDS membership. I did not feel that I belonged there or in any of the other groups I found.

The one big common denominator among all the left-wing organizations of the time, small or large, was opposition to the war in Vietnam. That was an especially burning issue among college students, because there was still a draft. It hung over the heads of all college men and all their girlfriends, and I used to say that you could not get three college students in the same room for five minutes without the subject of the draft coming up. It was never a popular war, and that made the idea of being sent half way around the world to fight and perhaps die or be maimed for an unclear cause especially abhorrent.

One of the most respectable institutions to oppose this war, as they had all others, was the Society of Friends, or Quakers. I somehow contacted a couple of women who belonged to the nearest silent meeting and they invited me to breakfast at their home one Sunday morning and to the meeting afterward. They had apparently had some connection with my family, and my father seemed to know who they were. He appeared a bit surprised that the people I had breakfast with were a couple of "old ladies," but it did not seem that strange to me. I have always liked old ladies. Anyway, I found the meeting very interesting. There was no formal structure whatever. We just sat quietly until someone felt moved to say something. After that, there was silence again until someone else spoke. I did not speak, at that or any of the subsequent meetings I attended. But one of the people who did stand up and talk blew me away at first sight.

She was older than I but looked younger and wore a long skirt in the "hippie" style of the time. And she spoke with an earnestness that forced me to listen to every word. Oh yes, and she was a redhead. I sought her out after the meeting and we got to talking and I learned that her name was Lucia, after the famous opera *Lucia di Lammermoor*. It was not that surprising a name, given her Italian ancestry, but she did not like it at all. We were joined by a man who suggested that we go someplace to eat lunch, and we did. I do not know whether he suggested that because he sensed that something was happening between the two of us, or what.

I remember only two things from that lunch, other than that I felt increasingly drawn to her. First, she said she was going away to college in a few days to begin a special program for older students who perhaps lacked some of the usual educational background. Second, she told me about a Marxist bookstore in the area. When we parted, there was little reason to think we would see each other any time soon, if ever. But she must have stayed on my mind, because the next day I found myself in the bookstore.

It was a pleasant little store run by a pleasant woman who appeared to be in her fifties or so and who was, as the expression went, a "card-carrying communist." I had some interesting conversation with her, and while I was there a couple of young men came in, one of whom brought a copy of a magazine called *Vibrations* that he was publishing and wanted her to carry. Then Lucia walked through the door.

Naturally we were both very surprised, and I, at least, was very glad. But I had a problem. The first meeting of one of my graduate history courses was going to start in about an hour. Not wanting this fortuitous reunion to be sabotaged by a mere academic obligation, I called the professor and asked if I would be missing a lot if I did not get to the first session. He said no, so instead of going to it I took Lucia to an Italian restaurant. From then on things developed fast and furiously. She went off to college and lived in a YWCA or someplace like that, and I visited her and became friendly with the couple that worked there as house parents or something.

When I visited her, the four of us went to an auditorium to hear George Wallace, the governor of Alabama. He was widely regarded as a racist and was running for president on his own American Independent Party ticket. Of course he never had a chance of winning, but Lucia was actually afraid that he would. In spite of her all-consuming interest in radical politics, she had very limited understanding of political realities, and her perceptions were shaped largely by fear.

I do not have a clear sense of the chronology during our relationship. One time when I went up to see her, I took her sister and brother-in-law with me. When we were going to leave, Lucia said she wanted to go home with us. I was very surprised. It meant dropping out of college, and I should have tried to talk her into staying.

Some time later, she told me that she had wanted to leave because she felt that if she stayed, we would never see each other again. I do not know why she thought that, but if she was right and if she had stayed, our inevitable breakup might have happened before we became engaged and been less painful for both of us.

We did get engaged, and we spent a lot of time in a house occupied by a group of young white women in a poor black neighborhood. Lucia identified strongly with blacks. During one of my visits while she was in college, I met an older man whom she had gotten to know at a huge civil rights demonstration in Washington, D.C., and who had become sort of a surrogate father to her. And then there was a poem she wrote called "What Shall Be the Color of My Soul?" The answer came in the last line: "Black." I told her I thought the poem would be more effective if she let the answer be just clearly implied, which it was, rather than explicit. But she insisted that the word "black" be there, perhaps lest anyone miss the point she was making about herself. I think she may have felt a little guilty about being white.

I am not sure just when our relationship began to deteriorate. We had begun to make plans for our marriage and a minister who was involved in various liberal causes was going to perform the ceremony. I think it was Lucia who first got cold feet and we postponed the wedding. But at some point I started to realize what a hopeless match we were and did not feel like making new plans. Things dragged on for some time, but finally one night she gave me back her ring and it was over.

Even though I guess I had seen the handwriting on the wall, it still hurt when it happened. I told Sam that it was hard to take because I had come so close to something wonderful, and he said no, I had come close to something horrible. He was right. There was a huge cultural and intellectual gap between Lucia and me that could never be bridged by what was really just my latest extremist attempt to fit in where I did not belong. I would keep trying, but could never be successful until I discovered who and what I was. And that discovery was still a long way off. For the time being, all I could do was to once again point myself in a new direction.

Sometime during the Lucia period, I had given up my history studies, dropped out of school for the umpteenth time, and started to write a novel. That was not really going anywhere, so I decided to go back to graduate school and back to English. I talked the head of that department into accepting me, and I started what would be the most successful phase of my post-high school academic career. I did not have a girlfriend and, like the time I left the hospital for good, I was ready to focus on my studies. I am not sure what my first course was, but it may have been Anglo-Saxon. Whenever I took that one, I found it fascinating. Although it eventually developed into modern English, it did so slowly and through intermediate steps, so studying it is virtually learning a foreign language. Also, my professor taught it phonetically, and that was the first serious exposure I ever had to phonetics.

Discussions with my father about that course and other academic matters helped to improve our relationship. The process was also facilitated by a softening of my political views. Basically, my loss of Lucia had resulted in the loss of the radicalism that had been a major bond between us. I now became a critic of socialism and even campaigned for a major-party gubernatorial candidate.

Anglo-Saxon was also how I met Julia. She was one of two women in the class and actually it was the other one whom I asked for a date. I only went out with her once, though. I think that was the spring term. In the summer I signed up for the research methods course, and when I went to the first session, there was Julia. I sat near the back of the room that day, as was my custom. But the next day I moved up to a seat next to her. For a couple of days we just talked after class, but one day when she had to pick up her five-year-old daughter at preschool, I asked to take them both to dinner. After that, we started dating regularly. By the time the fall semester started, we were already talking about marriage. The whole thing moved very fast, and that was largely my doing. I felt that my illness had taken a lot of time out of my life, and I was eager to make that time up.

Although some people are reluctant to marry a woman with a child, I liked her daughter, and I also liked the fact that when I got married I would immediately have a family. From the day Julia and I got married, I have always thought of Olivia as my daughter. We got married during the fall semester, and before long Julia was pregnant. That made me all the happier. Not only did I now have a family, but the family was already growing.

My family of origin was not exactly delighted. On one hand, since I met her in graduate school and she was from a middle-class family, she seemed a more appropriate choice than Lucia. But on the other hand, she was divorced, which did not sit well with either my Catholic mother or my nonreligious but nominally Episcopalian father. The Jesuit who had talked me into returning to college two actually recommended that we have a civil rather than religious marriage, perhaps so that in the eyes of the Catholic Church it would not be valid. But I had no intention of ever having our marriage dissolved, and for us the only reason for choosing a civil ceremony was that we had no reason to want a religious one. For my second marriage, the situation would be quite the opposite.

Julia dropped her courses when we learned that she was pregnant. In anticipation of the new member of the family, we started looking at houses. At the same time, I was trying to figure out where to go for a Ph.D. after I got my M.A., which should be in the spring. One of the places I was considering was Kent State University, later on the site of the infamous incident when National Guardsmen fired on a student demonstration, killing several people. Had I chosen to go, I would have been there at the time of the shooting, and since I was still strongly opposed to the Vietnam War, I might very possibly have taken part in that demonstration. Something like that reminds one of what dire unforeseen circumstances can follow from a seemingly harmless decision. I did not go there, and neither did I go to the local university that would have been the most obvious choice. I think one reason for that was that my old friend Carl had studied there for a while, in the same Ph.D. in English program that I would have been in, and had found it very difficult.

While Julia and I lived in that city, things went reasonably well for us. Olivia was in kindergarten and went to religious classes with Julia's nieces. In fact, we joined the temple, adding one more facet to my history of religious experimentation. I was finishing up my coursework for my master's degree. We saw quite a bit of Julia's family, but probably somewhat less of mine. I do not think my family ever fully accepted her, although that does seem a little inconsistent with my father's negative reaction when we decided to get a divorce.

During that period, as always, I was confronted with various examples of my difficulty in accepting traditional gender roles. I think that Julia had some very definite ideas of what men and women were supposed to be like and what their respective roles in a marriage were supposed to be. I could never understand such distinctions, and I do not think I ever met her expectations of a man. I do not think I even wanted to. And yet I do not believe her expectations were particularly unusual. I remember hearing similar ideas from other sources. One time I told my mother that I thought women should be able to become Catholic priests, and she said she thought there were some things priests had to do that women would not be able to handle. I did not ask for examples. I have always failed to ask a lot of questions that should have been asked.

My mother's comment stands in sharp contrast to the attitude expressed years later by another elderly woman in my family. I was at a large gathering of many branches of the family that my mother's health prevented her from attending. The only member of her generation was one of my aunts, who seemed very comfortable in the role of matriarch. During one event she seated herself at a table, and one by one the rest of us went over to pay our respects and chat for a few minutes.

When I sat down with her, we touched on politics and then somehow Catholicism came up. I knew that she was a very devout Catholic, but I ventured the opinion that, to survive, the Catholic Church would have to either let women be priests or let priests marry. I was as surprised as I was happy when that somewhat patrician old lady pulled herself up into an almost regal position and declared, "Well, I certainly hope they do *both*!" That was one of the first of many instances that have convinced me that the old, maybe especially old women, are often among the strongest voices for change.

Another example of my resistance to gender-role stereotypes around that time happened when I was talking with a couple of men who had attended a philosophy lecture with me at the university. I do not know how the conversation got around to marriage, but somehow the question of whether a husband should have the ultimate authority over a family came up. One of them, whose answer was clearly in the affirmative, thought the best analogy was that a ship can only have one captain. I do not think I said anything at the time, but later on I thought of two huge problems with that analogy. First, why on earth compare a marriage to a ship? And second, even if there did have to be a single boss in a marriage, why should it always be the husband? Clearly, I was already challenging certain prevalent assumptions about gender differences.

I became frustrated with the attempt to choose a house and decide upon a graduate school for pursuing a doctorate. Eventually, I avoided both issues by deciding to do something that Julia had wanted for some time: move to New York. She had lived there for several years, both before and after marrying her first husband. He was a writer of some repute, so they had considerable connections in the New York literary world of the sixties. Not that being there with me would bring her back into that. Even so, she considered New York an interesting place and our present city a dull place.

We flew to New York and hunted for an apartment. What we decided on was a new high-rise building on the Upper East Side. We went home to prepare for the move before returning to New York, where we lived in a hotel while waiting for our apartment to be finished. We hired a decorator recommended by an old college friend of Julia's, who lived across town. The decorating job cost what seemed like a lot of money to us, but that the decorator called a "tight budget." That, along with the rent we were paying (compared to what we had paid before) was a reality check about the cost of living in New York. Not to mention the issue of why anyone would *want* to live there with children. And we did have children, in the plural, our son Sean being born a few months after the move, in the same hospital where Olivia had been born six years earlier.

We soon learned that a common way of dealing with the challenges of raising children in the city was not living there all the time. We kept running into people who had a house somewhere in the suburbs and spent most weekends and summers either there or somewhere else away from the city. We considered doing that and looked at houses in Westchester County near another old college friend of Julia's. We spent a summer up there and enjoyed it, and I actually started liking the idea of living there full time. But Julia was not interested in that, saying she was afraid of the suburbs. I think she thought life there would be relatively isolated compared to the city.

Life in the city definitely had its high points. When we first moved there, I found it very exciting. It seemed to have everything there is to have and then some. Although I had thought of applying to one of the graduate schools there, what I had in mind when we arrived was to get involved in the peace movement. As I have said, the Vietnam War was on every young person's mind in those days. I found the local office of the Fellowship of Reconciliation, a longtime anti-war organization. They were doing draft counseling, which meant informing draft-eligible young men of the various legal ways that military service could be avoided. There were actually considerably more such loopholes than I or most other people had realized. I started getting involved in that program but had an argument with the director and dropped out. If I had a dollar for every project I have started but given up on. . . . Actually, my next endeavor was writing a science fiction novel, and I did finish it, but could not find a publisher.

Julia and I never did develop much of a social life in New York, outside of doing some things with her friends from college. We gave a couple of parties in our first apartment there, which I think she hoped would launch our social life, but that did not really happen.

One of the parties did help me get to know one of my cousins, whom I do not think I had ever met. Another person who came to one of them was my childhood friend Paul, who was then a lawyer with a New York law firm. The only other party that I remember giving with Julia was a reception for the Libertarian Party's vice-presidential candidate that we gave a couple of years later, after we had moved into a co-op on the West Side. By then I had become quite involved in the libertarian movement, but that is a story for the next chapter.

Even though there were good times, by the third or fourth year our marriage was seriously strained. It was on a trip to California that everything really fell apart. The day we were returning to Frank's house after some sort of side trip, we had a horrendous fight and I realized that divorce was inevitable. I told Frank and apparently he told my father, because later he told me that my father had said, "Why can't he ever think of his mother?" I quoted that line to my therapy group back in New York, and they all thought it was a very strange reaction. Although he expressed concern that my divorce would hurt mom, I think she was actually better at handling undesirable events than he was.

As divorces go, ours was reasonably amicable. We did not try to hurt each other, and we did not try to use our children to manipulate each other. I moved into an apartment and maintained regular contact with Olivia and Sean. We used New York State's legal separation provisions to avoid adversarial proceedings. That was quite an enlightened law for its time, providing essentially a no-fault divorce in which an entire settlement agreement was reached prior to a one-year waiting period. At the end of the year, either party could have the separation converted into a divorce. The process enabled a civilized dissolution of a marriage that simply could not work. Neither of us had to accuse the other of anything. The problem was simply that we turned out to be fundamentally incompatible. We did not care about the same things or want the same things out of life. Some time later, Julia summed up the situation very perceptively by saying it could never have worked because our values were too different.

I have had only two serious relationships since Julia. One lasted for a period of months and the other has run for thirty-seven years and counting. The first one took me by surprise. After all, I had been determined that Lucia was going to be my last redhead. But then Connie joined my therapy group. It soon seemed that something was going on between the two of us, and I fell in love before ever seeing her outside the therapy room. I actually told her so during a therapy session, and I think I asked her out as soon as the session was over. Or maybe after one of the next couple of sessions. I was trying to make a date with her for New Year's Eve. She turned me down, but she later told me that she had hoped I would ask her again. The next time I did ask her out, she accepted and we did go out.

Our relationship pretty much followed my established pattern. At first it was great fun. I do not remember much about what we did together, except for eating at quite a variety of restaurants. Mostly we just enjoyed being together. I do remember walking in together and sitting down together at the first group session following our first date. Another member's reaction revealed how obvious it was that we were now a couple. Realizing that it would not work well for the group dynamic if we acted as such, I moved to another seat.

After a while, true to form for me, things started fraying at the edges. I know that one time I hurt her a lot by not showing up for a play she was in. When she called to find out what was wrong, I said that I was so hungry that I had been literally unable to move. It was true, but her response was succinct: "Bullshit." Then I somehow forced myself to go uptown for a cast dinner after the play, but things were extremely strained for the rest of the evening.

I do not really know what brought our relationship to an end. She did say that it wasn't fun any more, just work. And she told the group that I had become "more neurotic." I think our different political views had something to do with it, too. One evening she invited another couple to join us for dinner, and the discussion turned to some political issue. It soon became clear that she was more on their wavelength than mine. We went to a few libertarian events, and she liked most of the people she met there, but she never really bought into the underlying philosophy. Ironically, it was at some libertarian dinner I took her to that I met Sue.

CHAPTER VI

THE FREEDOM QUEST

When I first met Sue at the libertarian event I took Connie to, she must have made an impression on me, because I can still picture the scene quite clearly. We definitely talked for a while and she told me about her former fiancé, a libertarian with whom I became politically associated later on. The ironic thing is that Sue has no memory of me from that event, but does remember Connie! Even so, that occasion seems to me to have been prophetic. There I was, with a woman whom I loved but who did not share my belief in libertarian principles, meeting a woman who did share that belief and with whom I would ultimately fall in love. That basic substructure of shared belief would, I think, have a lot to do with the success of our long-term relationship.

Our relationship was, in fact, so intertwined with our involvement with the libertarian movement that I can only tell the story of one in the context of the other. My libertarian story begins well before I knew Sue. Its roots extend back to reading Ayn Rand's novel, *Atlas Shrugged,* while I was in the hospital. I was so caught up in it that I signed a ceramic piece that I made with a dollar sign, which Rand apparently regarded as a symbol of an advanced civilization. I also used the ideas in that book to construct in my own mind the concept of a pro-capitalist type of anarchism. Some seven or so years later, I discovered that a good many other people had come up with the same idea and often as a result of reading that same book. I eventually read a book about libertarianism called *It Usually Begins with Ayn Rand* by Jerome Tuccille, with whom I became friends.

For the first few years after leaving the hospital, my politics floundered around somewhat haphazardly. At about the time that I was dating Lucia, I wrote a letter to one of my high school's publications, in which I described myself as "a sort of hybrid socialist/anarchist," but after our engagement self-destructed, I began to drift in a more conservative direction. By the time Julia and I were living in New York, I was reading the conservative magazine *National Review* and supporting the New York Conservative Party's candidate for governor. It was in *National Review* that I stumbled upon something that would change my life in some ways. It was a small classified ad for some libertarian organization, probably the Society for Individual Liberty. I wrote to them and they sent me a bunch of literature, which included a reference to Jerome Tuccille's first book, *Radical Libertarianism.*

After I read *Radical Libertarianism,* I was hooked. Since Jerry lived nearby in Westchester County, I called him up and introduced myself as a fellow "anarcho-capitalist." To explain the term, the "anarcho" part means opposition to any form of government. Most people think that anarchy means chaos and dangerous characters with bombs and probably some sort of voluntary socialism. But throw capitalism into the mix, and you have a whole different story, according to libertarians. Organization, opportunity, freedom.

None of that, of course, is what most people associate with capitalism, which has become pretty much a dirty word. But while others think of it as a form of exploitation, libertarians see it as a completely voluntary system in which each person is free to pursue his own best interest. That was the point of the popular book, *Free to Choose,* by the economist Milton Friedman. *Free.* To anarcho-capitalists, freedom is what it is all about. To them, government is the antithesis of freedom, because it makes choices for people instead of letting them make their own choices.

I want to emphasize that I am not trying to turn anyone into a capitalist, anarchist, libertarian, or anything else. I am only trying to show how certain ideas and activities played a part in both my personal journey and the bond that developed between Sue and me. The desire for freedom can be a powerful force for an individual, a group of individuals, or a nation (although it can mean quite different things to different people). It has always been important to me, and I think the search for it has strongly influenced the course of my life.

When people start talking about freedom, someone usually asks, freedom from what and to do what? It is certainly a fair question. For myself, I think that someplace deep inside, where I would not find it for a long time, the core answer must have always been freedom from gender stereotypes and to be the woman I really am. A basic principle of libertarianism is the right to do whatever you want as long as it does not violate anyone else's rights. This has to mean that I have the right to be what I am, whether or not other people like it or approve of it. I knew that libertarians uphold the right of gays to be who they are. Perhaps some still hidden part of myself realized that this would include a transsexual lesbian like me.

Back to my introduction to the libertarian movement. It was probably something Jerry Tuccille sent me that alerted me about a big libertarian conference at Columbia University. It was an amazing experience for me. There I found a whole crowd of people who thought the same way I did, but with enough variations to make it interesting. I think even Milton Friedman was one of the speakers, as was Murray Rothbard. Murray was an economist whom a lot of people thought of as "Mister Libertarian."

At least in my day, economics was the cornerstone of libertarian thought and the kind they embraced was "free market" economics. (That old freedom thing again.) Libertarians are almost obsessive about the market. They seem to think that if it is allowed to operate freely, without any interference by the government, the market will provide the best solutions for practically every aspect of life. A popular joke among libertarians went like this: "How many libertarians does it take to change a light bulb? None. The market will take care of it." At least we had enough sense of humor to laugh at that.

Seriously, though, a large part of the appeal of libertarianism (at least for me) was that it looked like a magic bullet that would solve every problem. We felt like a select group who knew a secret that could save the world from the irrationality behind most people's actions. In fact, the idea of understanding human actions provided the title of a book that libertarians may revere

as much as Ayn Rand's *Atlas Shrugged.* That book was
by the economist Ludwig von Mises, who exemplified
the Austrian School of Economics and was the major
force in bringing it to the United States. If Rothbard was
the guru, Mises was the source. His major work was
called *Human Action,* and as I understand it, he argued
that the tenets of economics (as well as other fields)
could be derived from a set of basic axioms about human
action. He called the study of human action "praxeol-
ogy." Austrian economics has never been accepted into
mainstream economics, but has long had a following
among conservatives and libertarians.

I left the Columbia conference in a state of excite-
ment. This libertarian business was what I had been
looking for. These libertarians were the *people* I had been
looking for. Maybe I had finally found a place where I
would actually fit in. I learned about something called
the New York Libertarian Association. I had the address
but apparently not a phone number, so I found the
apartment where it met and slid my card into the
founder's mailbox. On the back I wrote a note asking
him to call me. He did. One thing about the libertarian
movement in those days was that it was so small that
anyone in it jumped at the opportunity to find another
kindred spirit. And kindred spirits were definitely what
I found when I started going to the NYLA meetings.
Crammed into that little West Side apartment was probably the most intriguing bunch of oddballs I had ever
encountered. I loved them.

Before long I heard that someone out in Colorado
was starting a libertarian political party. That really got
my attention. Maybe I could stop flipping back and

forth between left and right. Libertarianism was a third
alternative. To perhaps oversimplify, libertarians are conservative on economic issues and liberal on social issues.
The best of both worlds, as we see it. I soon became
actively involved in the effort to develop a political party
that would promulgate this alternative to both liberalism
and conservatism.

My first contact with the Libertarian Party was a letter from Ed Clark inviting me to the second meeting of
the Free Libertarian Party, which was the name for the
party in New York State. I went and became involved
quickly, being placed on the State Committee. That
was at the time of our first presidential campaign, with
John Hospers and Toni Nathan for president and vice-
president, respectively. Julia and I hosted a reception for
Toni in our apartment. Unfortunately, the party was not
yet big enough or sufficiently organized to meet most
states' requirements for ballot access. I think we were on
the ballot in only two states.

I was not setting out to change the world, as some
fellow libertarians were. A popular libertarian slogan was
"Freedom in our time." I thought that was totally unre-
alistic. If what we meant by freedom ever came about, it
would not be in any of our lifetimes. So what did the
Libertarian Party mean to me? To be honest, it was
mostly a game.

Actually, the party was started at a time when I was
already designing a political game in my head. My idea
was to get a thousand people together and tell each of
them to sign up for one of four imaginary political parties: far left, liberal, conservative, and far right. The idea
was that they would offer various resolutions and form

coalitions or change parties in order to win the vote. The resolutions could be about anything, serious or comical. The point was not their merits, but the political process itself. I knew I would not be able to organize such a game myself, so when I joined the Libertarian Party, I hoped it would function in a similar way. Before long, I told my therapist that unless I could stir up some trouble in it, I was going to drop out. I wanted some controversy, not boring cooperation. In fact, when I applied for membership, I said the party should just endorse candidates of other parties. I had no interest in running our own campaigns. One time a party leader accused the members of not wanting a political party. He said what we really wanted was a debating society. That sounded good to me!

Controversy came soon enough. The state party wanted its own platform, and I was on the committee charged with writing one. And that brought us up against the biggest issue dividing libertarians: anarchy versus limited government. I was squarely in the anarchist camp. I thought as Thoreau did when he commented on the famous statement, "That government is best which governs least." Thoreau extended that dictum to its logical conclusion: "That government is best which governs not at all." Even while in graduate school, I was arguing that governments by their very nature relied on violence and coercion. So since the whole point of libertarianism is that society should operate on the basis of voluntary action rather than coercion, no government could be acceptable. The ideal society would be like one huge version of *Let's Make a Deal*.

I could not really understand the "limited government" position. First of all, most governments *are* limited. Only dictatorships, absolute monarchies, and other forms of totalitarianism wield unlimited power. Certainly the United States and other western democracies have limited governments already. The only question was where to draw the line. Just how limited do you want the government to be? Wherever you draw the line, it seemed to me, you would still be infringing on someone's freedom. And as a seasoned political extremist, I was not much into drawing lines anyway. I preferred the all or nothing approach. We anarchists did not think the "limited statists," as one of us called them, were really libertarians at all.

The limited government folks, of course, thought that we anarchists were off the wall. They had no problem drawing the line between too much government power and not enough. Most of them wanted the government to protect people against anyone who would violate their rights by force or fraud. And by rights they seemed to mean freedom to do whatever you want as long as you do not violate anyone else's rights.

So the opposing camps were pretty clearly defined. What we did to prevent the disagreement from tearing the party apart was to figure that we would work together until we got the government down to the size the limited government advocates wanted, and then fight over whether to get rid of what was left. But that did not solve the problem of how to draft a platform that we could all accept at least for the time being. The way I remember it is that I wanted it to avoid taking either side, but the limited government advocates insisted that it had to reflect their views. Of course, they may remember it quite differently. Either way, at some point I must have become convinced that there was no way to resolve the conflict. When the issue came before the membership at our state convention, I argued that we should just decide to do without a platform at the state level. That position carried the day.

Having achieved that rather strange sort of victory at the state level, I began to focus on the national party. I got elected as the representative from our region and went to the national convention. That was not a presidential nomination year, so the big event was the election of the next national chairperson. At that point I was also coordinating Jerry Tuccille's campaign for Governor of New York, and I put myself in an awkward position by supporting the candidate who was running against the one that Jerry and most of the other leaders of the New York party were supporting. I did it for a couple of reasons.

I met Philip because some our more radical members (whom I always somewhat sympathized with) were supporting him. I was quite impressed. He was young and somewhat charismatic and generally more colorful than the other guy. He was also Sue's former fiancé, though at the time that did not have much significance for me. I think what really got me to support him was that he asked me to second his nomination. I had already achieved something of a reputation as a speaker in New York, and a couple of his supporters told him to ask me. The opportunity to address the national convention was too much to resist. I wanted that audience. And as things developed, it turned into an even better opportunity.

Very early in the campaign, it became clear that my candidate was not doing well. For some reason, he and his supporters were looking like troublemakers to a lot

of the delegates. One of his supporters was Sue, but I
did not pay a lot of attention to her because I was dating
someone else and she was keeping a low profile in the
campaign. After a while, the man who was supposed to
make the nominating address dropped out. That was
great for me, because my guy asked me to do it. That
was much more prominent than the seconding address,
and I was raring to go. The morning of the election, he
told me that he was going to lose and lose big and
offered   to
let me off the hook about nominating him. Was he serious? Did he really think I would give up *my* chance to
address the convention just because *he* was going to get
clobbered?

I gave my address and the vote was taken. My candidate was trounced but my speech was good. Later on,
he wrote somewhere that it was the kind of speech that
would have made the difference in a close election. It did
a lot to elevate my status as a serious player in the Libertarian Party at the national level. It also made me aware
of an interesting fact about how I was perceived. A lot
of people have been surprised the first time they have
heard me speak in public. Apparently in more normal
situations I do not seem like the kind of person who
would be good at that. When one libertarian who had
not been at the convention was told that I made a good
speech, he turned to me and said, "I didn't think you
had it in you." I guess it was in me but it took special
circumstances to bring it out. Even before the national
convention, one of the New York party officers who had
heard me make three nominating speeches in the same
morning asked me if I had known previously that I could

do that sort of thing. I replied that yes, that is one of the things I know how to do. I have always known that, but for some reason others do not seem to expect it.

I think the way that people perceived me as a very different type of person in different situations says something about the conflict within myself over what gender I was. There were a number of indications during my Libertarian Party days that people had trouble trying to figure me out. At times I acted like part of the dominant faction, and at times I acted like a radical troublemaker.

Some people in the party may have thought I was two-faced. I suppose I really did have two faces in those days. One was the skinny guy with an unkempt beard and long hair that I saw in the mirror, and the other was the cute redheaded woman I saw in my mind. One time a party member remarked about the contrast between all the hair on my face and head and my relatively conservative suit and tie. He said, "His head doesn't match the rest of him." That is practically a definition of a transsexual! A few years earlier, someone had said that my Lincoln Town Car did not match my appearance or general presentation. Perhaps I subconsciously realized that two different identities were at war within me and found various ways to express that condition.

The dust settled from the convention and the New Yorkers went back to the Tuccille for Governor campaign. We had an ambitious goal: to get fifty thousand votes so that for the next election we would be put on the ballot automatically, rather than having to get thousands of signatures for a petition. The petition drive required an army of signature gatherers, both volunteer and paid. Then, after they were collected, the signatures had to be checked against the voter rolls. It was not easy for a minor party to get on the ballot in the State of New York. It *was* easy in New Jersey. So after collecting the comparatively few required signatures, several of the New Jersey party people came over to New York to help with the paperwork. One of them was Sue.

During that petition drive, Sue and I saw more of each other than we had before the convention. I found myself thinking about her a lot. I was no longer dating anyone, and I definitely wanted to ask her out. I had held off for a while because she was dating a friend of mine, but the point had come when I figured that all is fair in love and war, and I was ready to go for it. One night we were both at a bar that had become sort of a libertarian hangout, and we were in a small group of people playing an arcade game called Flash.

Someone came over and told me I should be in on some strategic discussion that was starting, but I had something on my mind that was more important to me than either politics or Flash. I have no idea who won the game, but I was after the real prize. When it was over, I told her I wanted to call her up and ask her out. She said all right, and I called her a day or two later. She said she did not expect me to do it so soon. Maybe she had not been sure that I was serious or that I would follow through. I was and I did. We made a date.

One of the boldest things the Tuccille campaign did was to produce and air a television commercial. That was very unusual for a minor party. It was a cute one, too. It showed a taxpayer walking past a row of bureaucrats at desks. Each one took something away from him until he had nothing left but his pants, and the last one was looking ominously at those. Sue played the first bureaucrat and grabbed his briefcase. She would be at the studio taping that commercial just before our first date, and I was going to pick her up there.

When I arrived, I apparently made a great impression on her by wearing a coat and tie. I had not thought anything about it, but it turned out that the man she had been dating before had refused to wear anything dressier than a T-shirt on weekends. As a result, he could never take her to a particular bar she wanted to go to. I could. The evening was great, and after that we dated each other exclusively.

Probably the first trip we took together was to Colonial Williamsburg, a place she had always loved. I met a couple of officers of the historic area and became quite interested in how it was run. We visited a lot of the restored buildings and just generally had a wonderful time. From then on for quite a few years, going there was an important thing that we shared together. At some point we joined a society of supporters, and during its annual meetings we had the chance to see a lot of behind-the-scenes workings of Colonial Williamsburg that were not accessible to the typical tourist.

Our relationship was personal and political all at once. Most of our travels during our early years together were related to the Libertarian Party. We were both on the National Committee, so we attended committee meetings and national conventions all around the country. At conventions we always had a suite and always threw a party. It was fun knowing people from all over the place and running into them all over the place. The Libertarian Party was our social life and it also gave us the chance to rub shoulders with people of much more prominence both in and out of the Party. And of course the political intrigue was a great game. One time when I said something irreverent about the Party, someone asked why I was a member. I answered, "Some people play chess; I play politics." Not a bad comparison, actually. After all, they are both games of strategy.

Another important part of our life was our families. For me, that mainly meant my children. They were with me frequently, as was Sue, so they knew her for quite a while before we decided to get married. They seemed to like her and she liked them. My parents also seemed to like her, which was gratifying because they had never been fans of either Lucia or Julia. I only remember one time when they visited us in New Jersey. I think I made it clear that we had a serious relationship but also that we were in no rush. I imagine the second part of that was especially welcome news, because my previous mode in affairs of the heart had usually been full speed ahead without much thought. Also, while we were out on the deck relaxing after dinner, I am sure Sue made a good impression on my mother when she showed her some pictures she had taken of Sean.

I got along well with Sue's family too, starting when I first met them. I still lived in New York, and driving to her parents' house in New Jersey was an eye-opening experience. I had a typical New Yorker's view of New Jersey: it was a strip of oil refineries along the Hudson River. As soon as I got far enough west to be in the small towns and countryside of Morris and Somerset Counties, I started to feel as though I had slipped through some portal into a land of fresh air, trees, and wildlife. It seemed like a nice place to live. I felt that way even more when I was in her house and met her family. I liked her whole family from the start and felt a particular rapport with her father. Many years later, at a memorial service for him, I recounted that he had made me feel that if I ended up being a part of that family, it would be a pretty good deal, and it has been.

I moved to New Jersey in 1976. It was a big year in several ways. For one thing, it was the year of the first coordinated, nationwide Libertarian presidential campaign. Although the Hospers-Nathan campaign in 1972 did not get very far, in a curious way it inspired the MacBride-Bergland campaign four years later. Roger MacBride had been a Republican member of the Electoral College in 1972 and had attracted attention by casting his electoral vote for Hospers instead of Ford. That made him an instant Libertarian celebrity and gave him a big boost if he wanted to be the candidate in '76. He did.

Another advantage Roger had stemmed from the campaign finance law at the time. The amount of money that any individual could contribute to a presidential campaign had been severely curtailed in the name of limiting the political influence of rich donors. There was, however, one exception: the candidate himself could spend up to fifty thousand dollars on his own campaign. Roger MacBride, a lawyer and television producer, was able to take advantage of that provision.

The MacBride campaign brought out some interesting cultural tensions within the Libertarian Party. For some libertarians, opposition to *laws* forcing people to live in certain ways seemed to spill over into resentment

of any individual or institution that expects people to
live in accordance with its standards, even if no coercion
is involved. Thus, some libertarians objected when
Roger MacBride wanted people wearing coats and ties
around him for a photograph. Similarly, in the early
days of the Cato Institute, the libertarian think-tank
originally funded by the Koch brothers, I heard someone complain that everyone in their Washington office
wore a three-piece suit. Too establishment, I guess.
Although I actually liked three-piece suits, I am sure
that the general desire for freedom from social con-
straints resonated with my inner need for freedom from
gender role expectations.

Disdain for social pressures seemed to result in a certain degree of social awkwardness. I fit right in, because
with my gender confusion there was no way I could be
anything *but* socially awkward. Another factor that did
not exactly foster the social graces was the prevalent ideal
of "rugged individualism," which could come across as
self-centeredness. This tendency was not necessarily
denied. After all, Ayn Rand praised egoism and wrote a
book called *The Virtue of Selfishness*. And Robert Ringer,
who wrote a book extolling libertarianism, had previously authored one called *Looking Out for Number One*.

Such was the emotional and ideological terrain to
be navigated by anyone wishing to represent the Libertarian Party as its candidate for president. Roger beat his
rival for the nomination by a healthy margin, but there
were a lot of bad feelings going into the vice-presidential
nomination. And that was where things got ugly. Roger
had his own choice for a running mate and apparently
thought he could get the one he wanted by vetoing any-

one else. But although the convention rules clearly gave him the right to veto, many delegates were incensed when he threatened to use it. We finally managed to select a vice-presidential candidate (not Roger's choice). But the New York delegation was badly split.

The half-dozen most outraged delegates tried to get one of their number elected regional representative from our region. I had not planned to run for re-election, but I decided on the spur of the moment to do so in order to stop the rebel candidate. When we caucused for that election, resentments were aggravated by the fact that two of the New York leaders commended me for my previous performance in that office. They said later that their comments were not intended as an endorsement, but that was how it sounded, even to me. As a result, my re-election turned the rift in our ranks into a veritable chasm.

For Sue and me, however, the most difficult event of the MacBride campaign came when we were flying down to a national committee meeting on Roger's converted DC-3. The flight took eight hours, but the bar was well stocked and it would have been great fun except for one thing. A couple of months earlier we had broken up for the third and last time, so we spent all those hours avoiding each other within the posh but not spacious cabin of that grand old plane. In New Orleans the ice thawed enough so that we were talking to each other. Then on the last night she went to Preservation Hall with someone else, and made sure I knew about it.

It was like a bucket of ice water poured on my head. I suddenly realized that she was not going to wait around forever for me to come to my senses. If I wanted her back, I had to make up my mind right then or risk losing her forever. When I asked myself what I wanted in those terms, I knew that it was not even a question. The next morning while we were both in line to check out of the hotel, I talked with her and we made a date for back in New York. I had already made plans to spend a few days with my parents, and I did. I felt very buoyant for the brief time I was with them, and very eager to see Sue.

Our first weekend back together was all anyone could ask for. I felt that the time had come to tell Sue the one secret I had been holding back. I had always known that at some point I would tell her about my time at the hospital but wanted to wait until she could see me as the person I now was rather than as whatever stereotype she might have about mental patients. The timing actually turned out to be perfect, because she gave me an ideal opening. She told me she had just learned that a friend had spent some time in a mental hospital. She had clearly been surprised that someone she knew and liked had had such an experience. She was definitely ready to hear my story, and she took it in a very understanding way. I knew that now our relationship was full speed ahead with no looking back.

I do not remember just when we decided to get married. Years later, when our children asked how I had proposed to mom, I had to admit that I never really did. One day I just said that it looked as though we should get married. She agreed, and after a while we started to make plans. I moved out to New Jersey to the same general area where she was still living with her parents, and we did our house-hunting together. Her father was transferred to California, and both her brother and sister moved out there too. By then her sister was married and I think it looked as though her father would be in a good position to help her husband get a job in the same large corporation he worked for. I am not sure why her brother moved, except that he did not have any particular reason to stay in New Jersey.

Sue had two reasons: her job and me. She moved into an apartment, and we never lived together until we were married. We were, however, more involved in each other's lives than ever. She was then chairperson of the New Jersey Libertarian Party, and of course I became active in it. I liked most of its members, but found them to be different from most of the libertarians I knew in New York. New Jersey was not the hotbed of anarchism that New York was. I also joined Sue's Episcopal Church. I felt very welcome there and quickly became involved with a small charismatic group. That worked out well for me because when I became religious in New York, I was attending a church in the Assemblies of God, a major Pentecostal denomination. (Pentecostalists and charismatics both place special emphasis on the direct workings of the Holy Spirit in people's lives.) I also liked the pastor, which was fortunate when we started making serious wedding plans.

CHAPTER VII

COUNTRY GENTLEMAN

Getting ready for the wedding was probably no more and no less hectic than for most couples. In spite of having been married before, I knew no more about wedding preparations than Sue did, since my first marriage involved only a judge and a couple of witnesses in a courthouse. Simple and to the point, no pomp and circumstance. What Sue and I had in mind was quite different. We were going to get married, as she pointed out, "in front of God and everyone." The religious part was very important to us and apparently to my mother, too. I was assuming that her sincere Catholicism would make her unhappy about both my divorce and my remarriage, but my father told me that the fact of a church wedding went a long way toward getting her to accept it.

My mother herself said something that did even more to help me understand her attitude. At one point when I mentioned the ceremony being held in an Episcopal church, she said that we might be able to do it in a Catholic church. I knew what she meant: since my first marriage was a strictly civil observance, the Catholic Church could take the position that it was never valid in the first place and that, never having been married, I could not be divorced either. I may not have the logic quite right, but she agreed with me.

I did have to explain that Sue and I were Episcopalians now and we wanted to get married in our own church. That was not what she would like to have heard, but I think she understood and accepted it. One question remained: how would our Catholic relatives react to the situation? I told her that if she let them know that she supported this marriage, they would come. She did, and they did.

One of the biggest issues surrounding most weddings is the question of who wears what, with the bride's dress being everyone's main interest. Sue answered that one in an unusual but awesome way: she made it herself, using an eighteenth-century style. She gave her bridesmaids a pattern either to sew themselves or give to a dressmaker. I went to a local men's formal wear shop, and at some point during the process of picking things out, I became so agitated that I started screaming at the shop owner. I apologized immediately, and he said he understood and that he had actually fainted before his own wedding. In addition to buying a tux for myself, I rented grey formal suits for my brothers, who would be best man and usher. When they saw them, Frank complained that they looked like livery outfits, and that what I got for myself looked much better, but Sam was cool with it. I think he understood that it was *my* wedding and I was *supposed* to look better than they did!

When the big day finally came, everything was just about perfect. I was very into all the ritual and even followed the old rule about not seeing the bride at church until the ceremony started. Almost everything went as it should, and Frank was a great best man, and everyone loved Sue's dress. The only hitch was that Sue and I completely forgot to kiss when we were expected to! So there we were, standing at the altar waiting for the pastor's wife to play the recessional, while she was waiting for the kiss.

Fortunately she gave up after a long awkward pause, and we got to march out of there and go to the reception at a nearby inn. That went well too, with a nice mix of relatives, church members, one libertarian couple, and an assortment of other friends. By the time we snuck out, changed clothes, and took off for our honeymoon, we were invigorated by the warmth of friends, family, our love, and the feeling that we were embarking on a wonderful new chapter of our lives.

When we returned home, we began that new life living in the same house I had been in since moving to New Jersey. We transferred from the Episcopal Church where we were married to one closer to home. We liked it, and Sue promptly joined the choir, which automatically made her an integral part of the church. I had no such easy entry into the active life of the church, and I have always somewhat envied the way singers are so quickly accepted into any congregation. I have always had a more difficult time feeling that I belong. One place in a church where I never feel I belong is the men's group. Even back when I assumed I was a man, I was never comfortable in groups that were for men only. I felt that I was out of place, without knowing why.

The next time we changed churches, it was part of a more comprehensive change. Although we had been pretty happy while living in our first house, it was never the sort of house we were going to want for the long term. We talked to an interior decorator about making

various changes, but before long we realized we were trying to turn it into something it just could never be. Then
one day I saw that an eighteenth-century house not far
from us was for sale and asked Sue if she would like to
take a look at it just out of curiosity. After all, we were
great fans of Colonial Williamsburg and loved the
restored houses from that period. Well, we took a look
and were immediately bitten by the old house bug.

About a year and fifty houses in five counties later,
we found what we were looking for. It was a big white
house on a few acres of land, and it was like none of the
others we had seen. Although the original section was
eighteenth-century, it had actually been moved,
enlarged, and modified in the early twentieth century
and had numerous design features characteristic of that
period. We had originally had something more exclusively typical of the earlier period in mind, but the older
and newer features of this house went together in a very
graceful and intriguing way.

It had been the main house on a large estate that was
subdivided around 1950, and it still seemed to me to
have the character of a manor house. So the new role I
tried on was that of a country gentleman. That one did
not fit me much better than the others I had attempted
to squeeze into, but it was definitely an interesting experience, especially because of the demographics of the area
where we were located.

Our area had its share of unremarkable people such
as ourselves, but it also had more than its share of the
rich and famous. Some nationally prominent government figures, a couple of the more colorful business people in the country, a major recording star, lots of people

in the horse riding and foxhunting world. One of the horse farms was actually owned by a king. It was a land where Mercedes-Benzes were commonplace and private schools were the norm. It was in many ways a white Anglo-Saxon Protestant paradise. Who needs diversity when you already have the best of everything? Living there inevitably made me ponder the nature of fame and fortune.

Whenever I hear that something has brought someone "fame and fortune," my sincere prayer is that it will also bring fulfillment. In our society, we tend to equate success with money. Even though people say, "money can't buy happiness," how many really believe that? Many certainly *act* as though they think it *can*. Some even say it. The interesting thing is that I have known a number of wealthy people in my life, and I have never heard any of *them* say that money can buy happiness. Some of them were happy and some were not. The happy ones seemed to know that their money was not why they were happy. And the unhappy ones *really* knew that money could not buy happiness.

During the first several years of our marriage, Sue and I were still active in the Libertarian Party. The year 1980 was an exciting one for libertarians. We had what may still be our most successful presidential race. Our candidate for president was Ed Clark, whom I had known since the very beginning of my experience in the party, because he was the first chairman of New York's Free Libertarian Party. Ed was a personable and credible candidate with an impressive educational and professional background. But the quality of the campaign was due in large part to his running mate. And once again the ticket was influenced by the campaign finance laws. A lawsuit, (in which I believe the Libertarian Party was involved,) had challenged the previous law as an infringement on the right of free speech. The result was that the national candidates themselves could contribute an unlimited amount to their own campaigns, while the amount that anyone else could contribute was still strictly limited. The ironic result was that campaign "reform" that was intended to curtail the importance of heavy financial resources in an election actually made it more important than ever to have a rich candidate. Enter David Koch, who, with his brother Charles, has become a major force in American politics. Though less well known then than now, they were libertarians and wanted to do the most they could for the Clark campaign. So Sue and I and every other delegate to the nominating convention received what may have been the most unusual letter in the history of American politics. It was from David Koch and said that he wanted to give several hundred thousand dollars to the campaign but that the only way he could legally do so was to be on the ticket. He went on to say that he would not be an active candidate. He was definitely not trying to buy the nomination, and I am quite certain that if he could have contributed that much without being the candidate, he would have done so. I will say, however, that the convention changed his mind about campaigning. In his acceptance speech, he said that he was going to learn how to make an impassioned speech like the New York delegate who had spoken in support of him. I am not sure he quite accomplished that, but he definitely ended up contributing more to the campaign than just money.

Not that we did not appreciate the money. Small, new political parties have little chance of growth without support from a large contributor. For that reason I think that restrictive campaign finance laws do more harm than good if the goal is to foster the free exchange of ideas, which strikes me as an appropriate goal for a democracy. David Koch's contribution gave us a much louder voice than we could otherwise have had, partly because its size escalated considerably from his original offer. By the beginning of the convention, the number that delegates were anticipating had grown to a million dollars.

Campaigns were not our only interest in the Libertarian Party. As Christians, we were acutely aware of the predominance of atheism, sometimes even militant atheism, in the party. I recognized at least two reasons for this. The first was simply the strong anti-authoritarian attitude of most libertarians, whether in or out of the party. That attitude extended not only to the government but also to religious authority and to the supreme authority. The difference is that while it might be possible to abolish government or at least severely limit it, if there is a God there is no possibility at all of abolishing or even limiting him or her (or it?). So, for those who reject any authority at all, it has to be assumed that there is no God.

The other reason that I am aware of for the predominance of atheism among libertarians is that so many of them embraced the philosophy of objectivism. This can hardly be a surprise, considering that its greatest champion was Ayn Rand. In fact, several of the New York libertarians I knew had been students of the Nathaniel

Branden Institute, which was founded and run by her chief protégé to promulgate her teachings. Some of us actually thought objectivism was a religion, with Rand as its guru, but dared not voice such a heresy around her followers.

So, surrounded by objectivists, many of whom considered their philosophy to be a necessary part of libertarianism, Sue and I decided to establish a haven for Christians in the Libertarian Party. We placed a small ad in a libertarian publication and invited other Christians to join us in starting a Christian Libertarian Fellowship. Then we started our own publication, a newsletter that we launched at the next Libertarian Party convention. We set up a booth at every convention for the next five years or so and even represented our fellowship at the first meeting of an organization called Libertarian International.

The newsletter progressed from quarterly to bi-monthly to monthly, and we distributed it free of charge to promote and publicize the fellowship and to develop our concept of Christian Libertarianism. The fellowship grew steadily and after a while we started a (very small) business to publish another, hopefully for-profit, newsletter. One question we had to deal with was what the purpose of the fellowship should be. We had always viewed it as having two purposes. The first was to support other Christians in the party, who often felt somewhat unwanted due to its generally anti-religious tone. The second was to convince the party that such a tone would greatly limit its appeal in a nation where so many millions of people still take religion seriously and believe in some sort of deity. On the other hand, the large anti-religious majority in the party thought our main focus should be on trying to turn Christians into libertarians.

The whole experience was very interesting and increased our visibility in libertarian circles. One time we were in South Carolina attending the Libertarian state convention and I ran into a man who was in town for the Republican state convention. We exchanged names, and when he heard mine he said, "You're a *big* Libertarian." I was quite amazed. I knew I was somewhat well known among libertarians, but I did not think anyone else would have heard of me. Then, just when we were gaining some visibility, I threw in the towel. I told myself, and others, that I was beginning to question my own belief that libertarianism exemplifies Christian morality in regard to interpersonal relationships. But looking back with my present understanding of myself, I have to think that it was largely just one more time that I gave up on something instead of carrying it to fruition.

As my radical libertarian activism slowed down and virtually ended, it became time to try on a new identity. I seemed to change identities the way other people change clothes. (For some people, changing clothes is part of changing identity, but more on that later.) This time it was the solid citizen, member of the establishment role. I had a good start on it, being an Episcopalian, and even when we became Methodists it was pretty much the same mold. Although I never gave up my life membership in the Libertarian Party, I became a registered Republican. I followed the stock market and took a bunch of finance courses and taught a course in financial management. And I joined the Rotary Club.

Rotary was an interesting experience. It started off

well, in that I became a member the same day that our club voted to admit women. So there I was, probably the first woman ever admitted to our local club, and of course no one knew it. But did I sense that there was something especially fitting about the timing? What I do remember is that I was very glad that particular day was when I joined. I seemed to be generally well received, and when the next president was elected, he asked me to be editor of the newsletter. I accepted the offer and most of the members seemed to like what I did with it. One advantage for a pretty new member like me was that people were always coming to me about something they wanted in the newsletter, so I got to know a lot of members quite quickly.

The new club president was also involved in something that did not work out as well for me. He was executive director of a local nonprofit social service organization, and their board chairman approached me one day at the club and asked if I would like to be on the board. I had never served on anything like that, and I liked the opportunity, so I said I was interested and they took me and yet another club member to lunch to discuss the idea. During that lunch I learned something that surprised and disconcerted me. It turned out that the organization was funded primarily by the government, usually to run specific programs that the government wanted.

I had expected that the programs would be conceived by the organization itself and funded by private donors. The heavy involvement of the government bothered me both because of my general bias in favor of small government and because, as the old saying goes, he who pays the piper calls the tune. I should have paid attention to my instincts and turned down the offer. This was not the only time that I have gotten myself into something despite my better judgment and ended up regretting it.

I did join the board, but I had been right to worry about so much dependence on government funding. I found an organization that was always jumping at the chance to run programs designed by someone else, instead of designing programs that best fit its own goals and vision. It seemed like a clear case of the tail wagging the dog. I was on the development committee (non-profit-speak for fundraising) and hoped to move the focus away from government funding and toward greater support from donors. But even the two other committee members, whom I liked a lot, said that if we were not receiving government money we should close our doors.

After a while such fundamental differences about how the organization should operate, together with a couple of other things I saw and did not approve of, convinced me that I did not belong on that board. I did not want to leave on a sour note, however. I stayed until my three-year term ended and then simply did not accept another term, despite the urging of a couple of other board members. This time I do not think I gave something up prematurely, but simply let go of something that was not a good idea in the first place.

The Rotary Club *was* a good idea, and even though I eventually felt that my membership was no longer useful to me, I do not regret it. And at least one thing that came out of it had good long-term results. A member who joined some time after I did was the assistant pastor at the local Methodist Church. At the time I was doing research on some theological issues, and we just naturally seemed to get along well. That came to pass about the same time that I was becoming disenchanted with our Episcopal church, and I suggested to Sue that we take a look at his church.

We went there one week to see the pastor and we liked him. Then we went to the Sunday service and we liked that. It was summer and we went to a picnic held out on the lawn in connection with the Vacation Bible School, and we liked that. Sue looked into the music program and she . . . well, you get the idea. We joined, and she sang, and I became involved in a healing service and a Bible study group. We met people we liked, including a man who would eventually work for us and whom we value as both an employee and a friend. Our children went to the Sunday school and made friends with some of the other kids. We felt pretty comfortable there. Until we did not.

One thing that became increasingly clear about that church was its homogeneity. Diversity seemed to be neither a fact nor a value. Almost all the members were white and middle class and most seemed to work for large corporations. Few seemed to have any strong roots in either the church or the community. One time I was talking with a pillar of the church and chanced to speculate about what our church would be like in ten years. He immediately responded that he did not care what happened to it in ten years because he would be retired and living in Florida. But what really showed us that we differed significantly from the predominant church culture there was the great organ battle.

When we first talked with the pastor, Sue asked if

the church had a pipe organ. He said no, but it would get one when the money was available. Well, the new pastor had different ideas. When Sue and I and a few others managed to raise enough money to buy not just any organ but a well-known and highly regarded instrument from a college that was closing down, he opposed it. He thought that in ten years the only music in churches would be "praise songs," and nobody would even know how to play a pipe organ.

It has been well over ten years, and I guess the young organists whom our new church has hired to play *its* pipe organ never heard his prediction. But the real issue was not how many organists there would be at what time. It was that neither the pastor nor most of the congregation at the old church thought they were a pipe organ kind of church. So we moved to one that was.

When we joined the church with the pipe organ, our son Todd and our daughter Lynne were ten and twelve, respectively. Although we were in regular contact with my son Sean and daughter Olivia, we did not start having our own children until we had been married about six years. I remember the births of Todd and Lynne clearly. With Lynne, timing was everything. When we were given the due date, at the end of March, I said to Sue, "It's going to snow that day." I had noticed since I moved to New Jersey that we usually got a big snow right at the end of March or beginning of April, and I did not relish the idea of driving Sue to the hospital in a snowstorm. And I was right: it did snow that day. But Lynne had come a week early, and we were safe, snug, and warm at home.

Although we did not have to drive in the snow,

Lynne did trick us a little on the actual day of her birth. Sue had a feeling that the time was imminent, so we put a plan in place. I had gone back to my boyhood hobby of ham radio, and I was supposed to attend a radio club meeting that evening. That was before the advent of cell phones, so we made an arrangement that if Sue felt the time had come, she would phone another ham in town and he would give me the news by radio.

I had a radio set to the right frequency but did not hear anyone calling me, so when I drove home I was assuming that this was not going to be the night. But a little later it looked as though it was, so we hurried to the hospital. It turned out that Sue's hunch earlier in the day had been right, and Lynne made her entry into the world.

Two years later, Todd had his own version of the keep-the-parents-guessing game. We had the day right, but when we got to the hospital, Todd seemed to be in no hurry. Thinking nothing was going to happen right away, the obstetrician went out to the hospital's garage to get something. Then, of course, Todd suddenly let Sue know that he was tired of waiting around and was coming out, doctor or no doctor. I dashed into the hallway and screamed very loudly that we needed a doctor *now!* A resident came running and got there just about in time to play catch. They had paged Sue's own doctor, but by the time she arrived, so had Todd. I turned to her and joked, "This is the best baby you never delivered." It had been a comedy of errors, but all's well that ends well, and both mother and baby were doing great.

With two young children now, our lives were exhausting, challenging, and good. At that point I was reasonably comfortable in the role of husband and

father, although I realize that I was unable to be a true
male role model for my sons. Even so, I remember lots
of good times we had together. We bought a pop-up
camping trailer while Lynne and Todd were very young
and took it to various campgrounds, especially one not
far from home that had a lake.

The longest camping trip we took was up to New
Hampshire one summer when Olivia had a job in the
Boston area. That was one of the times Sean went camping with us, so when Olivia joined us we had the whole
family together. That did not happen as often as I wish
it had, but we were often all together for Christmas, and
one year my parents invited us all to Tucson along with
my brothers' families. That was a great gathering and the
kids all had the chance to see some of my relatives whom
they had never met before.

Our most frequent trips around this time were to
Minneapolis. That was an old stomping ground for both
sides of my family, and we still had some relatives there.
We also had some business matters that took my brothers' families and my own to Minneapolis once a year,
and those gatherings served as annual family reunions
too. In addition, Minneapolis is simply a marvelous city
with many theaters, museums, and restaurants; an excellent symphony orchestra; and great special events; all in
an environment of Midwestern friendliness and helpful-
ness. (No, their chamber of commerce does not pay me
to say all these things, but maybe I should try sending
them a bill!)

We liked Minneapolis so much that for a few years
we rented an apartment there and went five or six times

a year. One of our favorite summer activities was the
Renaissance Faire held every year in one of the suburbs.
A couple of times, we drove north to the cabin on a lake
that had been in my family for decades and where I had
spent so many summers as a kid. Nor did we go to Minneapolis only in the summer. At least twice, we braved
the frigid temperatures of a Minnesota winter to go there
for New Year's Eve, which we would celebrate with a
concert at Orchestra Hall followed by a party at the convention center. Our trips up there tapered off as the kids
got older, and we let go of the apartment when we were
no longer using it enough to justify the expense. But we
still go up every summer for the meetings and family
gatherings. And Minneapolis also played a part in the
culmination of my path to self-discovery.

CHAPTER VIII

THE TRUTH COMES OUT

"I hate being a man," I said to the psychiatrist at our first session. She replied, "Do you hate being a man, or do you wish you were a woman?" I said, "Yes, I wish I were a woman. That's why I hate being a man!"

I had made the appointment because I had become aware enough of my gender confusion that for the first time in many years I thought I needed therapy. Of course I did not reach that state overnight.

For some time I had felt that there was something female within me that needed some way to express itself. At first I thought it was a desire to wear women's clothes, so I had been looking in the gay and lesbian magazine sections of Borders and Barnes & Noble, hoping to find something for transvestites or crossdressers. I had no success until one time I was in Minneapolis by myself for some reason, and I went to the Barnes & Noble. As usual, I looked in the gay and lesbian magazine section. This time I found something. It was a magazine called *Crosstalk,* which I thought was a very clever title. I took it back to our apartment and read it and found myself on a one-way street to discovering who and what I really was.

When I got home, I continued my research. It was exhilarating. I began to sense that I was finally uncovering secrets that had always lurked somewhere inside of me. In a book about crossdressing called *Vested Interests,* I saw an advertisement that began with an invitation to "be the girl of your dreams." Clever line. Somehow I found out about another crossdresser magazine called *Ladylike,* which was largely a place to see a lot of pictures of men dressed as women.

I also learned about Tri-Ess, a national organization for heterosexual crossdressers, which was how I thought of myself at the time. After a while, though, I realized that clothes were really not what it was about for me. Then I started thinking of myself as transsexual, that is, a woman in a man's body. I contacted an officer in Tri-Ess who happened to live not far from me, and we agreed to meet in a coffee shop.

When I met him, he looked like any other man around my age, since he was not "dressed." We talked generally about having a feminine side we need to express, and at some point one of us mentioned the classic phrase, "a woman trapped in a man's body." I said it did not really apply to me, because I did not feel trapped. We talked some more and then he asked me whether, ignoring the idea of being trapped, I felt like a woman in a man's body. When I said yes, he said that now he thought I was a transsexual rather than a crossdresser. Then he told me about a group of transsexuals in the area and said it would be interesting to see how they accepted me, considering that I did not make any effort to appear to be a woman. Until then, I do not think it occurred to me that one transsexual might not accept another one because of not seeming feminine enough.

From then on, I accepted that I was really a woman

in spite of my biology. But I had not yet reached that point when I started seeing the psychiatrist Dr. Flanagan. At that time I still considered myself a man and assumed that gender was determined by genitals. My feeling that it was impossible to be what I needed to be kept me in a state of turmoil. Sue knew what was going on, but not knowing what she could do for me was extremely frustrating for her. She could see that I was in great discomfort, and would ask what was wrong, and I kept responding, "I'm still not a girl." I could not see any solution to a very painful problem.

I knew extremely little about being transsexual except that I thought it required an operation, and I had no desire for that. Probably my first awareness of the surgery was in the 1950s when it was called a "sex change operation," and was brought to most people's attention by Christine Jorgenson. It was widely known as something done in Sweden. When my high school French teacher heard someone use a feminine pronoun instead of a masculine one, he loved to ask, "Did he go to Sweden?" I think I actually told Dr. Flanagan that I did not consider a man who had that operation to be a woman, but just a mutilated man.

An important issue in my therapy came up when I had a dream about a pretend wedding between myself and a little girl in my neighborhood when I was a child. I thought I remembered such a girl in the Minnesota town where we lived when I was between three and five years old. After that dream, unsettling thoughts about her began to fill my mind. Had she been killed or molested? One night when I had been asleep or at least trying to go to sleep, I suddenly bolted upright and cried out frantically, "Don't let it have been her. Make it have been me!"

Working on the theory that I had been traumatized back then, Dr. Flanagan encouraged me to try to figure out how. At her suggestion, I hired a private detective in Minneapolis to go to the town and investigate whether a little girl had been killed in the neighborhood while I was there. He suggested that I go there myself to see whether that would stir up any relevant memories. I did, and it was certainly interesting to see some old landmarks, but no new details surfaced.

My next step, probably also suggested by my psychiatrist, was to ask my brother Frank to meet me in Minneapolis because there was something I needed to discuss with him. I was much gratified that he did so on no more information than that. We had a very interesting conversation, and he told me that he thought he had some recollection of a little girl being killed and also that a little girl had lived in a neighboring house, but had no further details.

It also seemed very interesting, and a little eerie, that we both had dreams (or perhaps his was just an old thought) having to do with something troublesome happening in the space between the house and the garage. In my version, I was in that area and saw my father's gold-rimmed glasses lying on the ground, with the lenses facing upward. I do not know what that image meant to me at the time, but it has remained vivid in my memory for over sixty-five years. Yet since no one could come up with specific information, I thought we had hit a dead end. It would be some time before I realized that it was far from being a dead end.

Meanwhile, Dr. Flanagan and I explored some nightmares I remember from early childhood including, of course, the one I just mentioned. Because of the idea that I had experienced some traumatic event at the age of five or younger, she also consulted with a psychologist in the area who was known for having valuable experience in working with trauma patents. And then, when she informed me that she was moving to another state, Dr. Flanagan referred me to that same psychologist. I had seen her for two years. I would be seeing my new therapist a great deal longer than that.

When I started seeing Dr. Cohen, the question of the little girl who died was in the forefront, and before long I experienced a breakthrough revelation. *I* was that little girl. Although I was not physically killed, my existence as a little girl was snuffed out. When I told Dr. Cohen about this idea, she said she had always thought that the little girl might be me.

Although I do not know whether any one person played a primary role in convincing me that I could never be a girl, I think the job must have been done primarily by my family. After all, at such a young age they would have been pretty nearly my whole world. Although the result probably was traumatic, I do not blame any of them. They were part of a society and culture that knew virtually nothing about gender in today's sense of the word. Even Christine Jorgensen had not yet had her "sex change" operation. At that time the only thing that mattered was that I had male genitalia. Period.

Even after I realized that the little girl had been myself, I still had a strong sense that some particular traumatizing event had happened to me. Dr. Cohen and

I kept exploring the idea, and I kept hoping that some long-suppressed memory would surface and solve the mystery. That did not happen, and Dr. Cohen said that trauma did not always result from a specific incident. The working hypothesis we adopted was that I was traumatized by being forbidden to be the person I had to be. I think that was something of a relief for me, since it meant that I could stop searching for some villain who had done some horrible thing to me. Having reached that point, our focus now turned to the issue that the girl who was not allowed to exist is now a woman who knows she exists.

Now that I basically accepted the fact that I am a woman in a male body, a lot of work remained to be done. What exactly did it *mean* to be what I now knew I was? To many transsexuals it means changing their bodies through hormones and surgery and dressing and speaking and acting like women. I totally respect their decision, but I knew that was not what it means for me. That was the easy part. Figuring out what it *does* mean was the hard part. Dr. Cohen took me by surprise one day when she said I was "as full of stereotypes as anyone." That was not at all how I had seen myself. I had long been a feminist, even when I thought I was a man. I had long believed that women should not be limited by traditional gender roles. But as we continued our work, I began to understand what she meant.

The truth is that I have always struggled with various aspects of traditional gender stereotypes. I remember a conversation about sexism with a woman in the Libertarian Party. She said to me, "You're very good. Almost." On another occasion she caught me in the middle of a good example of the "almost" part. I was holding a car door open for her instead of getting in next to the girl I was dating. Little habits like that may be the hardest things to change. Even now it feels a little strange to get out of an elevator without waiting for a woman to go first, even if waiting might make it more difficult for her to get out! I am still very good. Almost.

Even though I am still not totally free of stereotypes, I did reach the point where I was reasonably comfortable as a woman in a male body. I realized that I was not a mistake. For me my condition was not a birth defect, although I understand why some transsexuals regard it as such. It was what I was always meant to be. If I had understood my gender when I was younger, would I have been interested in hormones, or surgery, or both? It is hard to say, especially since physical transition was at a less technically advanced stage and was less accepted and understood socially than it is now. And, of course, we still have a long way to go.

The important thing is not what might have happened, but what did happen. I overcame the great discomfort and distress that had previously plagued me because my true gender did not match my biological sex. That discomfort and distress is called gender dysphoria, and in my case it was overcome without medical intervention or any attempt to "look like a woman." I have no idea how many other people might be able to deal with being transsexual in the same way that I have. But I am sure I am not unique, and I believe that what has worked for me may be a viable option for some of the many other people who are struggling with gender dysphoria.

Moving beyond gender dysphoria did not free me from all of my gender-role tension. I still have to confront the same types of questions that many biological women are struggling with these days. To what extent would being a woman mean having to conform to female gender stereotypes? Many transsexuals feel a strong need to do this. I finally realized that for me freedom to be a woman did not have to mean giving up freedom to be myself. Before self-discovery, I never felt I could be myself around other people. If they knew who I really was, they would consider me unacceptable and reject me. Was the real reason why I felt I could not be myself that I did not know who "myself" was?

I remember being afraid to wear pink shirts. Would they reveal something about me that I could not admit to myself? At some point during my gender quest, I told Sue that my greatest fear was of being an effeminate man. I finally dealt with that fear when I was having an inordinately hard time trying to choose a new car. I was thinking about a German car known for its high performance, but I told Dr. Cohen that it was "boring." When I could not figure out why it was such a tough decision, she asked me one simple question: what color car would I want? My answer was instantaneous: "Pink, but I wouldn't have the guts to drive it." Then a light flashed on in my brain. The problem with the German performance car was not that it was boring. It was too stereotypically *masculine.* I wanted something more feminine, but that was a wish that I had always been afraid to indulge. Not any more.

Long-standing stereotypes are very hard to root out. I am still somewhat struggling with questions of what a woman can do or be. I identify as a lesbian almost as strongly as I identify as a woman. I find the idea of being a butch lesbian especially appealing, perhaps because they do not feel the need to conform to accepted roles for women. Still, I do not want to have to conform to butch stereotypes like flannel shirts and trucks, either. For a while I tried to figure out whether I was butch or fem, but then I realized that I did not have to be one or the other. I could be one way at some times or in some situations and another way at other times or in other situations.

I am always a little puzzled when people talk about dressing like a woman. Like *what* woman? The women with whom I most strongly identify are lesbians, and many of them dress about the same way I do. And what are "women's clothes?" These days skirts and dresses almost seem more popular with crossdressers than with even straight women, many of whom practically live in jeans and T-shirts.

So there I was, a trans woman who dressed "like a man," despite the fact that so many women dress that way too. I felt like an outsider even among outsiders. Some people might think that if I must have a gender opposite from the one that my genitals and chromosomes said I was supposed to have, I could at least do everything possible to make my body and appearance more like those of normal women. Well, I suppose that I do not do that because what I am trying to accomplish is to finally be what I really am instead of conforming to stereotypes. And as always, I am speaking only of my own experience and not telling anyone else what to do. Each of us has to find the way to deal with being transsexual that works best for him or her. If my experience can help anyone to do that, I will have accomplished my purpose for writing this book.

In my own process of dealing with being transsexual, I have felt the need to understand how my experience, relates to the broader society in which I live. My first way of looking at it was that I am a freak, but not in the ordinary negative sense of the word. I figured that if a woman with two heads would be a freak, so would a woman with a penis and Y chromosomes. I did not mean this as insulting in any way.

Quite a long time ago, I started thinking that "freak" could apply to desirable traits just as well as to undesirable ones. Thus Einstein would be a freak, and the world is probably a better place for it. So would Van Cliburn and some other child musical prodigies. I think that some athletes have been unique physical specimens and belong in the Freaks Hall of Fame. I think using the word "freak" this way might be similar to the way that some gays and gender nonconformists have started to call themselves "queer." After all, why should they let the word be defined by their detractors? If they are proud to be what they are, why not use the word with pride rather than allow others to define it as something shameful?

As I think about it, I realize that reclaiming words previously used in a derogatory sense has been done throughout history. As a Methodist, I especially like the way the word "methodist" was originally coined by John Wesley's detractors but later used by his followers. And to go even farther up the ladder of religious leaders, the word "Christian" was originally used negatively about the followers of Jesus but then used proudly *by* them. So with such lofty precedents, I was quite happy thinking of myself as a freak. Until I saw the movie, *X-Men: First Class.*

All the X-Men were mutants and each had some special power. My favorite character was Mystique, who was all blue, a shape-shifter, and a total fox. At one point she said she was "mutant and proud." You go, girl! So now I think of myself as a mutant. And proud. Think about it. In evolution, mutation is the process by which a species improves its viability and by which more advanced species develop. Indeed, some people are thinking that an understanding of gender fluidity could lead to a more advanced version of *Homo sapiens.* Be that as it may, I like the idea of being mutant and proud.

I did not like the idea of being anorexic. Sure, I have been underweight all my life, in fact, downright skinny, and not in the way girls want to be now. Some fifteen or so years ago, I met a girl who *was* anorexic, and she told me how lucky I was to be so thin. *Nobody* wants to be as thin as I am, unless they are anorexic. I had never *wanted* to be so thin; I just could not help it. And I did not have a distorted body image the way I thought anorexics did. When I looked in the mirror, I never thought I needed to lose weight. But one day Dr. Cohen said she thought I was anorexic.

Surprised as I was, I accepted the idea and thought it was because anorexia is primarily associated with teenage girls, and I knew that part of me wished I could be the genetic girl I never got to be in my own adolescence. But Dr. Cohen thought it was less about being a girl than simply about wanting to be little. I could not stop being tall, so the only way I cold be little was to be skinny. That does seem to make sense, because my wish that I could be a girl sometimes takes the form of being a little girl rather than a teenager.

One of the useful tools we used while the focus of my therapy was on coming to terms with my gender issue was dream analysis. For several years, I seemed to have dreams all the time and remember them fairly clearly. Of course my dreams covered all sorts of topics, and Dr. Cohen helped me understand their significance. But a theme that popped up all the time was about finding or looking for various types of locations. Often it was about finding new places that I did not know about before. Sometimes I would be in a building where I kept finding more and more rooms.

Dr. Cohen told me that rooms in a dream are parts of one's mind, which seemed very relevant, since at that time I was actively looking for things in my mind that I had not yet been conscious of. It was as though I was constantly searching for something, but always found new places to look. Sometimes the rooms would be in a very large house. Other times, in some sort of huge museum or art gallery where seemingly endless chambers were lined up one after another. A couple of times they were underground in some sort of cavern. I remember two especially odd versions. One of them was about a van or some similar vehicle, but it had two stories. And the other was about a single room, but it was inside the trunk of a tree.

In some of the dreams, the places I discovered were buildings rather than rooms in a building. I think what usually happened was that I would find one or more outbuildings on my own property that I had somehow forgotten about. And sometimes it was a whole town or housing development adjacent to or at least near our property. A couple of dreams were about finding an apartment to live in. The variations were endless, but the theme was the same: I was always finding new territory to explore. Which pretty well sums up what my therapy involved.

As in therapy, the searches in my dreams were not always fruitful. Sometimes I just got lost. That usually involved looking for my room in a hotel or college dormitory. Sometimes I would find myself going around in circles, and often the room numbers were not in any comprehensible order. That last problem also applied to the floor numbers in hotel elevators. The numbers on the panel would be all scrambled up, so I could not find the button I needed to push.

Sometimes the rooms I could not find were classrooms in either high school or college. Whatever the details, the point was always that I could not get where I needed to be. But in therapy I did get where I needed to be, or at least much closer than when I began. There are still some bits and pieces to pick up, but most of the heavy lifting has been done. And I no longer remember many dreams, perhaps because most of the exploration of my mind has been accomplished.

CHAPTER IX

PUTTING THE PIECES TOGETHER

There it is, right on the Great Seal of the United States: *E pluribus unum.* One from many. One nation formed from many states. Each state has its own separate identity, and yet together they form a single nation. This chapter is about the way "states" of another sort combine to form a different kind of entity. They are called "ego states," and several of them together can form a complete human personality while continuing to have their own separate and distinct characteristics.

The idea of separate segments within one personality was around throughout the twentieth century. By the 1980s, a number of therapists were writing about how they were using the concept of ego states in their own therapies. But the breakthrough event that enabled this approach to become an established form of psychotherapy came in 1997 with the publication of *Ego States: Theory and Therapy* by John G. Watkins and Helen H. Watkins. Helen Watkins had already presented their basic ideas in an article the previous year ("Ego-state Therapy: An Overview" in *American Journal of Clinical Hypnosis*). That article, and what I have learned and experienced in more than ten years with my therapist, provide the basis of this chapter.

At this point more than ever, I must emphasize that I am not a psychologist and that this book is about my personal experience. I realize that I may have misrepresented some of the Watkins' views and have almost certainly oversimplified them. In addition, ego-state theory has without a doubt been modified and developed in the last twenty years. But my own perception of the subject and my gradual awareness of my own ego states have been very valuable parts of my process of self-discovery.

There is one point that I feel must be addressed at the outset. Most people have heard about "multiple personalities." Actually, that term has been largely replaced by the term "dissociative identity disorder." At first it can be difficult to understand the difference between dissociative states and ego states, but it is an important distinction. Dissociative states, sometimes called "alters," can be thought of as separate personalities that control a person at different times. When one of them becomes overt and takes control, the "main personality" does not remember what happened while the alter was in control.

Ego states, unlike dissociative states, are parts of a single personality that is always present. Those different parts can express themselves at different times, but when one of them becomes overt, the personality as a whole remains aware of what is happening at the time and remembers it later. Even so, a person may not always be aware of which ego state is being expressed through a particular thought, feeling, or action. By increasing the awareness, people can better understand the reasons behind their behavior and gain more control over their lives.

Part of the normal development of personality is the

process of differentiation, by which we learn at a very young age to mentally separate a broad category into separate components. For example, a child learns that "clothing" encompasses shirt, pants, socks, and so forth. This process can also be applied to perceiving segments of one's own personality. When the differentiation process produces "discrete segments" of the personality, they are called ego states. But when various parts of a personality become excessively separate and "maladaptive," the resulting condition is known as "dissociation." There is a continuum from normal differentiation to the extreme dissociative condition called "dissociative identity disorder."

In the context of treating dissociative states, Watson emphasizes trying to make their boundaries more permeable so that they can communicate with each other and become "adaptive ego-states." Such ego states can maintain their separate identities while functioning as segments of a single personality. As an example of this process, she describes a patient who had moved from dissociative states to normal ego states. One of them expressed itself by saying, "We aren't separate persons anymore. We are just parts of her."

While an ego state may develop as a result of normal differentiation, another possible cause is trauma during childhood. A traumatized child may develop an ego state as a survival mechanism, and it may continue into adulthood as a separate part of his or her personality. Such an ego state will remain suspended in time, still thinking like the traumatized child. It can have a negative effect on the whole adult personality unless it learns how to be a more constructive part of it.

However they are caused, a person's ego states, taken together, compose a "family of self," or "internal family system." But it is not always a happy family. Covert ego states can conflict with each other, causing anxiety, depression, or physical issues such as eating disorders. Resolving the conflicts involves a sort of family therapy in which the ego states are encouraged to communicate with each other. If they remain covert, hypnosis may be used to activate them.

In my case, hypnosis was not necessary. I became aware of several young ego states, one by one. Each of them represented a different aspect of myself, and all of them, together with more adult aspects of my personality, definitely composed an internal family system. The first and youngest was the little girl whom I thought had been killed when I was about five years old, but whom I later identified as myself at that age.

I feel very strongly that at a very early age I was aware at some level that I was really a girl, but that as a girl I was "killed" in the sense of not being allowed to be one. When I realized that my awareness of being a girl had been suppressed for decades, I finally accepted the fact that she was still alive as a part of myself and named her Annie. At first she expressed only terror, but eventually she started to experience some of the joy of the happy childhood that she had been denied.

Thinking about Annie usually reminds me of a movie I saw not too far from the time I first discovered her. It is called *Ma Vie en Rose* (*My Life in Pink*) and I just love it. The main character is a seven-year-old boy who is certain that he was supposed to be a girl and has a funny fantasy about how God made a mistake with his chromosomes, replacing an X that went astray with a Y. He loves girls' clothes and makeup and puts his parents in an embarrassing position with their rather straight-laced neighbors and his father's boss. As a result they move away and he becomes friends with a very tomboy-ish girl. It is a very sweet movie and I recommend it.

After a while I became aware of another part of myself, whom I thought of as an older version of Annie. I named her Annie II and conceived of her as ten years old and a biological girl. Unlike Annie I, she was a happy little girl right from the start. She was also just about perfect. In my mind I modeled her after Alice, my child-hood friend whom I always thought of as more a sister than a girlfriend. I have always realized that Annie II was too good to be true and an idealized rather than realistic concept of what it would be like to be a little girl. She is also quite stereotypical, liking such things as dolls and fairytales and traditionally girlish clothes. That is actually rather curious, since Alice, while like that in many ways, also had a tomboy side.

Perhaps at the point when I became aware of Annie II, I still thought a child had to be "all girl" or "all boy." I think she has developed over the last few years and become more of a three-dimensional individual and less of a stereotype. That brings up an important point about my ego states: They do develop. Annie I is no longer so terrified that she cannot have any other characteristics. As I discuss my other internal family members, I will try to include some observations about how they too have changed since my first awareness of them. About the only thing that cannot change is their age. A new one can emerge who is basically a different-aged version of another one. But they will both remain separate and distinct parts of me.

The next girl to make her presence known in my family of self (and they are all girls except for one) was a sixteen-year-old genetic female whom I call Leigh. She is the first one old enough for sexual orientation to be a major issue, and she is clearly, consciously lesbian and glad of it. Girls seem to be the main thing on her mind. She thinks of herself as more fem than butch, but has a pretty strong sense that she can be whatever she wants. Like most teenage girls today, she spends about as much time as possible in jeans and T-shirts, especially ones with some sort of lesbian image or slogan if she is someplace where she can get away with it.

Leigh is not out to her school, but she is to her parents, who are generally accepting, and to a small group of friends, both gay and straight. She has a definite predilection for redheads, and her musical taste runs more toward pop than rock. She is basically my fantasy of myself if I were sixteen and had no Y chromosome.

Of course what I actually was as a teenager was a girl in a boy's body, but I did not know it. Leigh has a counterpart who *does* know it. Her name is Lisa. She is seventeen and fully aware that she is a girl despite having male anatomy. As a woman content with having a male body, I consider Lisa to be me as an adolescent. Like Leigh, she has parents who know what she really is and are accepting. In fact, Leigh and Lisa have the same parents, because they have come to know each other and actually think of themselves as sisters.

Like all of my ego states, Leigh and Lisa started out essentially isolated. They were aware of each other's existence but did not "know" each other. They also knew they were parts of me. In fact, Leigh once told my therapist, "I know I am part of Leigh Anne, but I don't want to be. I want to be my own self." As another example of how my ego states are able to develop, Leigh now seems to be all right with being part of Leigh Anne, which is my private name for myself as a whole. (The only people who ever call me that are my therapist and my wife.)

One interesting thing about the relationship between Leigh and Lisa is that I have a tendency to think of Lisa as more butch and Leigh as more fem. But why? The only explanation I can come up with is simply that Lisa is a biological male. But I do not want to think that way. I decided some time ago that as a whole person, I can be either butch or fem at any given time. So why should I expect Lisa to be any different, especially having just said that Lisa is just me at a younger age? Perhaps this paradox simply illustrates how complicated the whole issue of gender is. All any of us can do is to make as much sense of it as we can and not expect to be perfectly consistent all the time.

I think the last member of my family of self to surface in my consciousness was a ten-year-old whom I call Chip, which was actually my nickname at that age. She is Annie II's counterpart in the same way that Lisa is Leigh's counterpart: she has a boy's body but eventually realizes that she is really a girl. But at first she thought of herself as a boy who wanted to be a girl but never could. As a result, she was frustrated and unhappy, until Dr. Cohen suggested that Leigh Anne could explain to her that she really could be a girl even with a boy's body.

Now Chip is quite happy and has become friends with Annie, giving both of them a playmate. They understand their relationship with each other and seem to feel that they complement one another.

So there it is, the lineup of all the girls in my family of self, some with girls' bodies and some with boys' bodies. That leaves just one more young ego state who is part of my total adult personality. I call him "the Phantom," because he never really existed even though he was the only one who was "supposed" to. He was the boy everyone thought I was, including me, but who I could never be. He was the kid who had the bow and the BB gun and the .22 rifle and played basketball and football with the other kids in the neighborhood and built radios and wired the outhouse so a light would go on in the cabin whenever someone sat on the toilet seat.

Not that a girl couldn't do all the same things, of course. But in the 1950s, especially in a small southern town, they were not the sorts of things expected of a girl. The phantom was also the one who had elaborate fantasies about being a knight in shining armor or a mysterious young stiletto-wielding adventurer. I think of him as twelve, but he is really the boy I was supposed to be at any age. He was the sexist, stereotypical boy of the 1950s. He does not represent what I really was, but what I was supposed to be.

One day in March of 2012, I suddenly got some important insights about the girls in my internal family system. The trigger was the web series *Out with Dad*, about a teenage lesbian and her struggles to understand, accept, and communicate her sexuality. It had a very powerful impact on me (almost bringing me to tears), as such stories always do. This time I asked myself *why* stories about teenage lesbians always hit me so hard. My first answer was that part of me wishes that *I* had been a biological girl and had those experiences myself. Next, I realized that this part of me has a name: Leigh. And that Lisa is the part of me that is glad I was a biological male, so I could have Sue and my children. So Annie II and Chip, both ten years old, represent the same two parts of me, but at a younger, pre-adolescent, less sexual stage of my life.

It was not until the next morning that, with my therapist's help, I figured out what the Phantom is all about. He had always been the hardest one to understand. But now I realized that he is a part of me that actually wishes I had been the boy, psychologically as well as biologically, that everyone including myself thought I was. After all, it would have made my life much easier. But it was extremely difficult for me to admit that *any* part of me wishes that I had been a boy. Even though I have admitted it, I am still not really comfortable with that part of myself. Writing about him here has also been extremely difficult. For what seemed like forever, nothing I wrote about the Phantom seemed to ring true.

Eventually, again with my therapist's help, I realized that I did not know what to write about him because I did not know what I thought or felt about him. Making peace with the Phantom is still a work in progress and, in truth, so is the entire process of putting together all the pieces of myself. It is probably not a job that will ever be finished, and finishing it should probably never be the goal. It is a process of development, and development is not something to be stopped. It is something to be continued.

Even though I do not fully understand my young ego states, they benefit me as an adult. One way is that when I am very upset about something, I can sometimes deliberately bring one of them, usually Leigh, to the forefront. Because whatever my adult self is so worried or frightened about is not her concern, at times she has been able to function when as Leigh Anne I have been so upset that I literally could not move. Another way is by helping me figure out why I have a particular reaction to something. A prime example began when I saw a performance of the Puccini aria "O mio babbino caro" on the television show *America's Got Talent*. It was sung by a ten-year-old girl named Jackie Evancho and stunned viewers across America, making her literally an overnight star.

That performance had an immediate and overwhelming impact on me. As soon as I thought about it, it was obvious that this was largely because I was hearing her and seeing her through the ears and eyes of another ten-year-old girl, namely Annie. Annie idolized her. She viewed her as a little girl might view a young princess. And Jackie showed Annie that even a little girl could do amazing things. Since Annie is part of me, Jackie's effect on her soon prompted an adult reaction in me. It sparked an interest in opera.

In spite of stunning people when she sang a Puccini aria, Jackie Evancho insisted that she was not an opera singer but a "classical crossover" singer. I had never heard that term before, but it provided a link for Annie's reaction to her to "crossover" into Leigh Anne's response. I got on the Internet for explanations of "classical crossover" and examples of other singers considered to be in that category. At first I was attracted to that genre itself and thought I had finally found a kind of music I could relate to, being in between pop and classical. That led me to Vittorio Grigolo, who himself had just crossed over from classical crossover to opera. Soon I was hooked. We went to *La bohème* at the Met, and I finally shared Sue's love of classical vocal music.

Jackie Evancho has a consistent theme of following one's dream. Her first album, issued privately before she became famous, was called *Prelude to a Dream*. Talk about prophetic! When asked how she felt after a song on *America's Got Talent*, she said it was so amazing that her dream was coming true. When asked by someone what advice she would have for other young people, she said, "If you have a dream, follow it. It might come true." It did for her, she added.

Her first commercial album was called *Dream With Me* and makes the dream theme explicit with both the title song and "When You Wish Upon a Star." And one of the four additional tracks on the deluxe version is "The Impossible Dream." Her dream theme awakened optimism in me, spurred my desire to finally really follow a dream, and became one of my inspirations for writing this book. Optimism seems to be a common ingredient of youth, and one that is often lost in adulthood. Maybe getting in touch with the childlike part of yourself and realizing that it *is* still part of you can revitalize your optimism.

If Annie helped me to understand the powerful effect that a young musical prodigy had on me, it was another ego state who shed some light on my response to the sudden stardom of someone in the political sphere. When John McCain put the spotlight on a previously rather obscure governor by naming her as his running mate in his 2008 presidential campaign, my initial reaction was quite positive. But when my therapist questioned how I could find a clearly anti-gay candidate so appealing, I saw her point but did not have an answer.

She acknowledged that Sarah Palin was adorable, which seemed to be a widespread opinion of her, and suggested that perhaps I was seeing her through the eyes of sixteen-year-old Leigh rather than as my politically savvy adult self. I thought about that after the session and realized that Dr. Cohen was right. Simply put, Leigh had a very big crush on the adorable governor of Alaska! And once again my understanding of one of my ego states had rendered my otherwise surprising reaction quite comprehensible.

One Sunday afternoon, the New Jersey Symphony Orchestra played Gershwin and Grofé, both of whom were childhood favorites of mine. They swept me back to my childhood with an irresistible force. Once there, I began shaking uncontrollably, face to face with the dark side of that childhood; face to face with all the frustration, unfulfillment, emptiness, and loneliness that had begun there and followed me through the decades no matter where I went or what I did. Frustration. Unfulfillment. Emptiness. Loneliness. I spontaneously thought of the acronym FUEL and realized that those powerful negative emotions had indeed been the fuel that powered me through most of my life. Then I realized that if I wanted to replace that negative force with any sort of positive energy, I would first have to confront it. I believe that I am doing that now.

Throughout my life, I have kept returning to my youthful hobbies of stamps, coins, and electronics as a way to be in contact with my childhood, but my interest never lasts very long. Perhaps I am finally able to let go of them because getting in touch with my young ego states has provided me a more satisfying connection with my childhood. Not only does my adult self, Leigh Anne, accept the younger parts of myself now, but they themselves are becoming more aware of each other and more able to function together as parts of a single person without losing their separateness. This is an extremely important process for me, because I always used to feel very fragmented, as though different segments of my life had little to do with each other. Now I am finally beginning to feel like a whole person, thanks in no small part to identifying, understanding, and coming to terms with my various ego states.

CHAPTER X

THE GENDER SPECTRUM

My personal gender experience exists within the total context of gender as it is now understood. Now that gender is no longer seen as being the same as sex, it can be viewed as an entire spectrum comprising endless permutations. While sex is physical and therefore limited by biological realities, gender is psychological and limited only by imagination, which ultimately has no limits. There is a simple explanation of this that goes, "Sex is between the legs but gender is between the ears." Gender is one case where thinking it can make it so.

This is a relatively new way of looking at gender, and it requires vocabulary that will be unfamiliar to many people. And to make it even more complicated, that vocabulary is still in a state of flux. Many of its terms do not yet have universally accepted meanings. Some have different meanings depending on who is using them. In this chapter I am going to define a lot of terms, but I know that some of them are defined differently by some people. In those cases, I shall attempt to explain why I have chosen a particular definition. In at least one case, I will introduce a term that may be my own invention, because I use it for something that I do not think has previously had a name.

Since I am discussing gender in the context of how it differs from biological sex, the first term to define pertains to sex itself. The term, one of many that I had probably never heard prior to my own gender explorations, is "assigned sex." It refers to the sex the doctor writes down after delivering a baby. It is either male or female, and usually it is very easy to determine just by looking at the newborn's genitals. But not always.

More often than most people realize, the genitals are actually somewhat ambiguous, not being what are usually found in either a male or a female. The correct term for such a person is "intersexed," but the doctor still has to write down either male or female, so a decision must be made. Traditionally in such cases the female sex has been most commonly designated, and surgery is frequently performed to make the baby's anatomy more closely resemble what is generally associated with the assigned sex.

Because of being so subjective, "gender" is considerably more difficult to define than is sex. It is usually thought of as a combination of behavioral, cultural, and psychological traits that is typically associated with one sex or the other. The crux is the word "typically." What is typical in one nation, religion, class, or racial or ethnic group might not be typical in another. And even what is typical in a given context is only typical, not universal. An individual can perceive herself as more like most members of the other sex than of her own. What is most important for the individual is gender *identity*, meaning whether she self-identifies as male, female, or even something else.

If gender is not something objective like biological sex, what causes a person to identify as a given gender, especially if it is not the one usually associated with his or her assigned sex? Someday there may be a scientific answer based on variations of brain structure, nervous system, endocrinology, or some other physical characteristics. Research is being conducted in such areas. But for now, to me the only answer is expressed in a line from the classic blues song "Stormy Weather." In the words of the songwriter, "Something deep inside cannot be denied." That is ultimately the reason that I know I am a woman. And perhaps that is why I have always loved that particular old song.

Most people, of course, self-identify as the same gender that usually is associated with their biological sex. Most biological males consider themselves men, and most biological females consider themselves women. A fancy word for such people is "cisgender." I only learned that term a few years ago, and it still does not seem to be in very common usage. In the case of cisgender women, a catchier term is quite commonly used on the Internet. It is "GG," and when I started seeing it I was quite puzzled. When I asked someone online what it meant, I was told "genetic girl."

In our society, and probably virtually all others, men and women have traditionally been expected to play different roles. A few of these differences, most notably childbearing and breastfeeding, are pretty much dictated by nature. Some others have grown out of typical, but not universal, natural differences. Some jobs seem generally more suitable for men because men typically have greater physical strength. This difference, of course, has become less important as more and more heavy labor is done by machines. On the other hand, men have traditionally also been thought to be more mechanically inclined and therefore better at operating machinery. But in that regard, there is the constant question of whether one sex has done better at something because of greater innate ability or because of different socialization.

Many differences in traditional gender roles seem to be quite clearly little more than social conventions. For example, women have probably cooked more meals and made more clothes than men, but traditionally most professional chefs and tailors have been men. That discrepancy, along with many others, probably stems from the general social convention that women belong in the home, and men belong out in the workplace. And of course an even broader general assumption has been that men should have authority and women should accept men's authority, whether in a marriage, a business or profession, or government. Fortunately, these traditional distinctions have become increasingly blurred during the last fifty years or so.

When I was a student at an Ivy League university it was, like all the others, for men only. But it was closely associated with one of the top women's colleges, whose students were just as smart as we were, took many of the same courses as we did, and seemed to do as well in them. I remember thinking it was very strange that most of them were still expected to become housewives, while we were expected to basically run the world.

Now women are about as likely to become doctors and lawyers as men and are making great strides in business and politics. And yet there seems to be a "glass ceiling" making it very difficult for women to rise to the highest levels in these fields. When either women or men are highly successful at things previously reserved for the other sex, some people question whether they are "real women" or "real men." The reality is that expected gender roles are becoming less rigid but are still present and can still cause real problems for those who challenge then.

There are a couple of terms that pop up frequently in gender discussions that can include the concept of gender roles but have broader meanings. "Gender expression" refers to a wide range of characteristics that, in a given culture, are generally associated with a given gender. It includes occupation, interests and avocations, and aggressive or passive personality types. It includes gender "cues" such as facial hair, body shape, and voice. It includes clothing style, hairstyle, jewelry, makeup, and patterns of speech.

It must be emphasized that what these things express in regard to gender depends primarily on the cultural context. Trousers might be perceived as masculine in one culture (or subculture) but gender neutral in another. Particular types of jewelry may be considered feminine in one but not in another. Such things tend to be perceived as appropriate for a specific gender whether they are intended that way or not. But when they are deliberately used for the conscious *purpose* of being perceived as a member of a specific gender, they may be referred to as gender "presentation." This term is often used when someone is trying to appear to be the gender opposite his or her assigned sex.

The most general term for people whose gender expression differs from what is usual or expected of someone with their assigned sex is "transgender." It is useful as an umbrella term covering a broad range of gender issues, but its usefulness is also limited by the fact that it can be unclear just what is meant in any one reference. It is currently used so much that it may be difficult for people to understand the differences among the various types of people to whom it is applied. Ambiguity can stem from the fact that many of the people said to be transgender are actually cisgender, meaning that however much they may appear to defy usual gender expectations, they actually self-identify as the gender usually associated with their assigned sex. One group of this type, perhaps the largest, is the crossdressers.

Crossdressers are men who dress, usually only part-time, in women's clothes. The term is applied only to men, because these days it is perfectly usual for women to dress in traditionally male attire. And by the same token, crossdressers usually wear skirts and dresses and other clothing traditionally associated with women even if not the type of clothes that many actual women may prefer. A crossdresser can choose just how far he wants to go in the process of imitating women. The only common denominator is that almost all crossdressers see it as a means of expressing their "feminine side."

It has become quite popular to think of everyone as having both feminine and masculine sides, no matter which is dominant. Crossdressers like to think of their feminine side as a distinct persona, often with many typically female attributes. Some wear a completely female couture, complete with high heels. They make varying efforts to appear to have female figures. This usually involves some sort of artificial breasts, which may be anything from a bra stuffed with tissues to rather expensive silicone breast forms intended for women who have had mastectomies.

Some crossdressers go farther and get padding for their thighs and buttocks. Wigs and fingernail treatments often round out the transformation of appearance, while voice modification, mannerisms, and style of walking can all contribute to the overall illusion of femininity. For crossdressers who go to that much effort, the goal is to pass as women. Whatever they do in the process of "transformation," crossdressers usually give their female persona a typically female name, sometimes a feminization of their real name. Also, when "dressed" they refer to each other with female pronouns.

Another word that has the same literal meaning as crossdresser is "transvestite." That is actually the term I was familiar with in my youth, and it was generally used with a negative connotation. Crossdresser seems more common now and seems to be used with less disapproval. Actually, the idea of men dressed as women and trying to pass as such has long been used for comedy in plays and movies, including classics such as *Some Like It Hot* and *Charley's Aunt.* In those cases, the characters were not portrayed as actual crossdressers but as men who dressed as women for some specific purpose.

More recently, a few films like *To Wong Foo, Thanks for Everything! Julie Newmar* have portrayed gay men who dress like women simply because they want to. Such men, especially if they do it as performers to entertain others, are known as "drag queens." There are also lesbians who dress as men to entertain, and they are sometimes called "drag kings." I would say that all such activities are examples of crossdressing, even though the motivations and purposes may differ.

While crossdressers of any type deliberately express characteristics associated with the gender opposite their assigned sex, "androgynous" people have characteristics of both genders and may not be clearly perceived as either male or female. There are also people who do not self-identify as either male of female. Such people may feel that they have no gender, or some gender other than male or female, or all possible genders, or anything outside of the traditional binary model. I have not yet heard any names or definitions of third, fourth, or fifth genders, but that will probably come. The current term for anyone who self-identifies as something other than male or female is "genderqueer." (It should be noted that people within the lesbian, gay, bisexual, and transgender community now often apply the word "queer" to themselves, reclaiming it from those who use it as an insult.)

While androgyny creates some ambiguity about a person's gender, there is another term that is gaining popularity describing people whose gender may be clear but who act in some ways contrary to what is generally expected for that gender: that is "gender non-conforming." I consider it to have the broadest meaning of any of the terms we are examining here, and to encompass all the others and more. It could refer to appearance, vocation, avocation, taste in entertainment, mannerisms, or anything else that is socially linked to one gender or the other.

Our society still pigeonholes a lot of things according to gender. There is yet another term reserved for people who deliberately do something that defies gender expectations in an obvious and unmistakable way, for shock value or to make a point or both. That term includes a very rude word, so I shall substitute gender "violators." Whatever you call someone who does that, the classic example is a man wearing a beard and a dress. I once saw someone doing that at a gender conference, and even some of the crossdressers seemed taken aback.

Most of the versions of transgender people that I have discussed so far are actually cisgender, that is, they self-identify as the same gender that is normally associated with their assigned sex at birth. They are "trans" only in the sense that their appearance or behavior crosses over the line between what is typical for men and for women. The focus of this book, however, is on transsexuals, who can reasonably be included under the transgender umbrella but differ from the other examples in a crucial way. At the present time, there is no universally accepted definition of "transsexual," but most definitions fall into one of two general categories.

The simpler type of definition is that transsexuals are people who self-identify as the gender opposite their assigned sex at birth. The other type usually begins the same way but adds that the person has had or wants to have medical treatment, usually hormone therapy and sex reassignment surgery, to modify his or her body to conform more closely to his or her true gender. This type of definition is consistent with the belief, now being challenged, that such measures were the only effective treatment for what was called "gender identity disorder." But a problem with any definition that includes physical change is that it leaves out an important part of the gender spectrum. It ignores the possibility that someone who identifies as the gender opposite from his or her assigned sex may accept that situation without physical change.

I favor the first type of definition, but I think that something has to be added to allow that at a given time a transsexual may not yet consciously self-identify as his or her true gender. It does not seem logical that becoming aware of one's true gender suddenly changes it from what it was before. Full awareness may be simply the culmination of a long process of trying to figure out what makes one feel so different from other people with the same assigned sex. For that reason, I define a transsexual as someone who self-identifies, consciously or subconsciously, as the gender opposite the sex he or she was assigned at birth. For some, the self-identification may consist of a feeling that is not yet fully understood.

Now that we have defined transsexual, we can proceed to distinguish among the various types of transsexuals. The first distinction is very simple. A transsexual whose assigned sex is male but who self-identifies as female is called male-to-female, often shortened to MtF or M2F. One whose assigned sex is female but who self-identifies as male is female-to-male (FtM or F2M). Another and perhaps simpler way to express this distinction is that a male-to-female transsexual is a trans woman and a female-to-male is a trans man.

When someone realizes that he or she is transsexual, the inevitable question is, "Now what?" What do you do when your gender identity, which society considers to be perhaps the single most important thing about you, is turned upside down? For many, the answer is to change themselves so as to more closely resemble people whose gender is the same as theirs but matches their assigned sex. The process of doing this is called "transition," and it can take various forms. There are, however, two basic categories: social transition and physical transition.

Social transition is about living in the way that is generally associated with people of the same gender. It requires at least an attempt to be perceived as a member of one's own gender. That implies looking like a cisgender man or woman, and this is done in much the same way that crossdressers do it, as I have already discussed. Clothes, makeup, wigs, mannerisms, voice modification, and so forth. For female-to-male transsexuals, it may involve "binding" to make the breasts less prominent and "packing" to create the illusion of male genitals inside one's trousers. But successful social transition can require more than that. It may involve broad patterns of behavior, such as different ways of relating to men and to women. It involves "fitting in" with men or with women. The very fact that social transition does not involve physical change necessitates creating the illusion that various physical features are like those of cisgender people.

Almost all transsexuals who want to transition at all will try to achieve social transition. Many also feel a strong need to have their bodies be more like those of cisgender men or women. There are two main ways to do this: hormone therapy and sex reassignment surgery, commonly called SRS. I will give a little basic information about both, but please understand that nothing in this book is intended as medical advice. A doctor is needed for that, and even the basic information is subject to change as knowledge and procedures for treating transsexuals continually develops.

Hormones by themselves can have dramatic effects. For FtMs, injections of testosterone cause two changes that are major cues for one's gender. One is the growth of facial hair, and many FtMs deliberately grow a beard, which automatically says "man" to most people. The other is deepening of the voice, which can also send a strong signal of masculinity and is caused by thickening of the vocal chords. Additional effects of testosterone injections include cessation of monthly periods; enlargement of the clitoris; and increases in body musculature, sex drive, and red blood cells.

For MtFs, estrogen treatments promote breast development, and of course breasts are a major signal that someone is female. Estrogen treatments also decrease the size of the testicles, the prostate, and sometimes the penis. There is a decrease in sexual function, sometimes causing erectile dysfunction. Another effect of estrogen on trans women makes it especially important for them to be certain that they want physical transition at least to the extent achieved by hormones. Estrogen usually causes sterility, which usually becomes permanent after several months. At that point even discontinuing the hormone treatments will not usually restore fertility. It is also important to understand that the desirable effects of hormone therapy are *not* permanent unless treatments are continued on a regular basis. In addition to their physical effects, hormones can also affect a person's attitudes, feelings, and behavior. Overall, the changes they produce are enough for many transsexuals. Many others, however, feel a great need to have their bodies changed to a greater degree. For them, the only way to satisfy that need is through sex reassignment surgery.

For male-to-female transsexuals, the chief component of SRS is modification of the genitals. That involves
removal of the testicles, but the penis is usually not
entirely removed. Instead, its tissue is inverted and used
to form a vagina, and part of the head of the penis is
used to form a clitoris. There are, however, a number of
other methods that can be used to construct female genitalia. Some trans women have additional surgery such
as breast augmentation, facial plastic surgery, and voice
feminization surgery. Whether or not an MtF's transition
includes surgery, she is likely to have electrolysis or laser
hair removal (or both} at some point. Facial hair especially, no matter how closely one shaves, is a strong indi-
cator of male biology. Some trans women also choose to
have body hair removed in various areas, and for those
who do want SRS, removal of hair on the genitals may
be strongly recommended or even required.

For female-to-male transsexuals, the most common
form of SRS has been "top surgery." This involves both
removing breast tissue and reducing and moving the are-
olae and nipples. Several different techniques are available, depending largely on the size of the breasts and the
elasticity of the skin. Other FtM surgeries may include
removal of the uterus and ovaries. Construction of a
functional penis (called phalloplasty) has been more
challenging than vaginaplasty for MtFs, but great
progress has been made in recent years. It involves graft-
ing tissue from another part of the body and may
include a penile implant to facilitate rigidity, as well as
other associated surgeries.

Transsexuals sometimes describe themselves in terms
of whether they have had or intend to have SRS. They

speak of being pre-operative (pre-op), post-operative (post-op), or non-operative (non-op). Non-op, as I was surprised to learn, means not simply that someone does not want SRS, but also that he or she *has* had hormone therapy. There is really no term for a transsexual who wants no physical transition at all. That may be because many people still equate transsexual with physical transition.

In reality, physical transition is not what makes someone a transsexual; it is something that a person who is already a transsexual may choose to do as a way of dealing with being transsexual. It may not be a necessary choice or even the best choice for all transsexuals. In fact, the same can be said of social transition. For that reason I am suggesting a term that I have seldom if ever seen: "non-transition transsexual. " Not only does that term describe me, but also I believe it can perform an important function by filling in a serious gap in the gender spectrum.

In addition to being a transsexual, I am also a lesbian. To me, that is almost as important a part of my identity as being a woman. Sometimes the term "translesbian" is used. But it is important to understand that a transsexual's gender identity and sexual orientation are two separate things. A transsexual man or woman can be either straight or gay. Discovering that we are trans does not usually change which gender we are attracted to. A trans woman who was attracted to women when she thought of herself as a man will probably still be attracted to women when she discovers that she is really a woman herself. She was really always a lesbian, but did not realize it before.

On the other hand, a trans woman who was

attracted to men before will probably still be attracted
to them. So if she had thought she was gay when she
thought she was a man, she will now realize that she is
really straight. And it works the same way for trans men,
but in reverse. If all of this seems confusing to someone
who is cisgender, imagine how confusing it can be for a
trans person, especially for one who is just beginning to
understand his or her true gender identity. But, as with
one's gender identity itself, understanding and accepting
one's true sexual orientation becomes more comfortable
with time.

As I said at the beginning of this chapter, gender terminology is in a state of flux. So are the attitudes of mental health professionals concerning gender issues and
questions of gender identity. There are two main sources
for the currently prevailing views on these subjects. The
better-known one is the *Diagnostic and Statistical Man-
ual of Mental Disorders*. This is the closest thing there is
to a bible for psychiatrists, psychologists, and others in
the mental health field, and the latest edition, known as
DSM-5, came out in 2013. On the subject of gender
identity, DSM-5 is significantly different from the earlier
editions. The key change is that it has dropped the term
"gender identity disorder" (GID) and replaced it with
"gender dysphoria."

At first glance this change might appear to be just a
substitution of one bit of psychobabble for another, but
it is actually hugely important. Gender identity disorder
meant that self-identifying as the gender opposite one's
sex assigned at birth was in itself a mental disorder. But
gender dysphoria refers not to such self-identification
itself but to the *distress* it sometimes causes. Thus the

DSM now acknowledges that a transsexual (though it no longer uses that word) can be mentally healthy if his or her condition does not cause distress.

Although the fact that the DSM is published by the American Psychiatric Association gives it great influence among mental health professionals, there is a more specialized document called *Standards of Care for the Health of Transsexual, Transgender, and Gender- Nonconforming People*. Version 7 was published in 2011 by the World Professional Association for Transgender Health (WPATH), which was originally the Harry Benjamin International Gender Dysphoria Association. The committee that prepared the revised version said that "We've made a clear statement that gender nonconformity is not pathological." Similarly, the outgoing president of WPATH stated that in Version 7 the Standards "allow for a broader spectrum of identities—they are no longer so binary."

The SOC offers guidelines for the care of "transsexual, transgender and gender nonconforming people." Its goal is to "maximize their overall health, psychological well-being and self-fulfillment." To accomplish this goal, it promotes a broader understanding of gender health than has previously been typical for mental health professionals. For example, the SOC cautions therapists not to promote a binary interpretation of gender. This is important because the traditional viewpoint that a person must buy into either the traditional stereotype of a man or the traditional stereotype of a woman has made it very difficult for many people to simply be themselves.

The SOC defines transsexual as referring to "individuals who seek to change or who have changed their

primary and/or secondary sex characteristics through
feminizing or masculinizing medical interventions (hormones and/or surgery), typically accompanied by a permanent change in gender role." Its discussion of
transition, however, is less rigid. It calls transition "the
period of time when individuals change from the gender
role associated with their sex assigned at birth to a different gender role." But it acknowledges that this does
not always mean adopting the lifestyle generally expected
of the opposite gender. Instead, someone may find some
other "gender role and expression" best suited to that
particular person. And, very significantly, the process
may, but does not *necessarily* involve medical intervention. The emphasis is on the highly personalized character of transition.

My reaction to these definitions is mixed. Of course
I do not accept the definition of transsexual that requires
physical transition or the desire for it. What is needed,
that the SOC definitions do not provide, is a term for a
person who identifies with a gender different from his
or her assigned sex but neither alters nor desires to alter
his or her body to conform to his or her gender identity.

But I do like the acknowledgment that transition
does not always involve such measures. I also like the
idea that transition does not always have to be from one
of two genders to the other. This suggests a greater fluidity of gender than is allowed in the more binary model,
in which everyone is either clearly male or clearly female.

On the other hand, I think that the SOC puts too
much emphasis on gender role. A good example of what
I see as an excessive focus on gender roles is another pas-
sage in the SOC, which refers to "living part time or full

time in another gender role, consistent with one's gender identity." This implies that the SOC still makes the old assumption that only certain "roles" are appropriate for a given gender. It does not seem to allow for the possibility that for some people gender identity may not have much to do with any "role." I know that my self-identification as female has nothing to do with playing any particular role in society. In fact, for me the point is freedom to be myself rather than having to be what others expect from someone with either my assigned sex *or* my gender.

Even if the SOC exaggerates the importance of gender role, the real significance of Version 7 is that, like DSM-5, it takes the position that the mental disorder is not being transsexual but the distress that some transsexuals feel. It points out that "being transsexual, transgender or gender nonconforming is a matter of diversity, not pathology." So why the distress? At the root of gender dysphoria are social expectations and cultural norms that are expressed as prejudice and discrimination. Those are the causes of the distress, not the simple fact that an individual's gender identity does not conform to his or her assigned sex. Such pressures can cause psychological problems like the anxiety and depression that are common among transsexuals. But these problems, like other forms of psychological distress caused by society and culture, can be treated. And with treatment some transsexuals can overcome gender dysphoria without hormone therapy or sex reassignment surgery.

CHAPTER XI

LIVING INCOGNITO

So here I am, after all those years spent discovering my true gender identity and learning how to live it, walking around appearing to be all the things our society seems to value the most. Straight. White. Male. Well, I am white. The rest of it is all smoke and mirrors. Window dressing. Most of the time and in most places, I travel incognito. As a kid I loved stories about spies and other people who go around seeming to be somebody they are not. Incognito. But I never thought I would be cast in that role. Unlike a spy, I do not do it to deceive people. I do it because I am content as a woman in a male body and feel no need to broadcast that I am really a woman to people who have no need to know.

I call myself a woman in a *male* body rather than a woman in a man's body because I do not want to support the idea that one type of body is for men only and the other is for women only. One of the main points I want to make is that a person of either gender may have a body of either type. Since most men have bodies with one type of reproductive system and most women have bodies with the other, it is understandable that society calls the one type a man's body and the other type a woman's body. The many exceptions are made to feel that there is something wrong with them. But there is nothing wrong with them. The reality is that there are men with female bodies and women with male bodies. My male body is not a man's body. It is a woman's body. *This* woman's body.

And yet I "present" as male. I look male, sound male, and probably even walk and move like a male. Like a *man,* in most people's eyes. I even *call* myself a man when the occasion requires it. One of my least favorite things to do is filling out forms that require me to check off an "M" or "F" or a "Mr.," "Miss," or "Mrs." I know that they mean biological sex, but they probably think that is the same as gender. If I checked off "F" or "Miss" or "Mrs.," it would cause great confusion and, in some situations, possibly get me accused of misrepresentation or even fraud. So I check "M" or "Mr." and feel like a liar.

There is another situation that requires a public declaration of one's sex that is the bane of many transgendered people, not just transsexuals. Whether you call it a bathroom, lavatory, loo, W.C., restroom, men's room, women's room, little boys' or little girls' room, or anything else, it spells embarrassment, confusion, fear, and discomfort for a lot of people who do not fit society's definitions and expectations. It is even a problem for school children who do not feel that they are the gender usually associated with their anatomies.

Personally, I use the men's room to avoid trouble even though I feel that I do not belong there. Except for one place. At the Philadelphia Trans Health Conference in the Pennsylvania Convention Center, they always provide not only men's rooms and women's rooms but also "gender neutral" restrooms. Those seem to be the most

popular ones at that conference. I know I make a beeline
for one of them when nature calls. It is great to be able
to do what must be done without lying about what I am.
It is also quite an experience, seeing people of every
known gender (and probably some unknown) coming
in and out nonchalantly, without fear of anyone else's
reactions.

In addition to being unable to use the appellation
or restroom that would feel right for me, most of the
time I have to censure my speech to avoid saying things
that would feel appropriate to me but cause confusion,
unwanted curiosity, possibly verbal attacks, and conceiv-
ably physical attacks. I am talking largely about casual
or humorous remarks like "We women have to stick
together," or just the exasperated exclamation, "Men!"
At other times it might simply be a factual statement
about something I bought in a women's clothing store
or liking one thing better than another because it seems
more feminine.

Since I have to be so careful about what I say around
most people, there is a real sense of freedom when I am
with people who know who I really am. Sue was of
course the first to know. Then came my children, whom
I told individually over the course of several months. It
was a relief to be able to speak freely with them. The circle expanded when I came out to my brothers, and it
was very gratifying to be able to tell them that I am really
their sister.

While opening up to my own family, I was also
developing an expanding circle of other people with
whom I did not have to censure what I said. They were
primarily people I knew in various organizations that

support full equality for LGBT people, especially in a religious context. Since I have always been a very verbal person, being able to talk to people freely is a very important part of being myself.

I do not just present as male. I also present as straight. And since I consider being gay to be almost as important a part of my identity as being female, being perceived as straight is as much part of living incognito as being perceived as male. I am a lesbian presenting as a straight man. Incognito to the second power? Of course appearing straight involves different elements from just appearing male. The former depends mostly on clothes, body shape, facial hair, and voice.

Appearing straight is largely a default. If a man does not come across as stereotypically gay, he is assumed to be straight. I think I fall into that category for the most part, although I may have a few mannerisms, style elements, and interests that could raise questions in some people's minds. But I also have two things that enforce the straight assumption: a wife and children. Although most people know that some men with wives are actually gay and that some have children, both are still perceived as strong indicators of heterosexuality. So I am usually assumed to be straight.

But I am a lesbian. I have always been attracted to women and there was no way that being a woman myself was going to change that. I almost think that it has *increased* my capacity to love a woman. I cannot help thinking that love between women is the ultimate form of human love. I relate to lesbians better than to anyone else except my wife. I like to know them, see them, read about them, and watch movies about them. I know a good many and they are among my favorite people. There is one in particular whom I consider my model lesbian. If I want to think about what lesbians are like, I visualize her. But not all the lesbians I am familiar with are real people. A lot are fictional.

I am especially interested in young adult books with lesbian characters and themes. The idea was new in the 1980s, but by now there are a lot of them and new ones come out every year. They have helped many girls sort out their confusing and often unsettling feelings about other girls. They usually involve two high school girls who fall in love and at least one of whom is struggling to understand feelings she has never experienced before.

These books also help me vicariously experience the life that part of me feels that I was cheated out of. In fact, to further simulate that experience, I have been toying with the idea of writing a young adult novel or short story myself. I even have an idea for it, which is to make both girls ham radio operators and have them meet on the air. I could use a subtlety in ham jargon to help them realize the way they feel about each other, But for now that idea has to wait on the back burner while I work on this book.

Of course, not all lesbian-themed books are intended for teenagers. Adult lesbian literature spans many genres, from comedy to romance to detective stories and much more. Lesbian music and movies constitute another facet of the creative side of the lesbian world. For me, the arts are an important element of my identification as a lesbian. After all, the very word comes from the island of Lesbos, where the ancient poet Sappho educated young women in literature and love.

My sense of being cheated out of my girlhood is assuaged to a considerable extent by my young ego states, especially Leigh and Lisa. Leigh makes it possible for me to feel like a genetic teenage girl who is attracted to other girls. When I allow myself to think and feel like her, I can identify with the girls in the young adult lesbian novels and mentally and emotionally live in their world for a little while. Leigh can most thoroughly identify with those cisgender storybook girls, but Lisa adds another dimension for me. Like me as Leigh Anne, she experiences being female in spite of having a male body. Between the two of them, they provide me with a type of link to my youth that I was missing before I discovered my true gender.

Another one of my young female ego states, Annie, gives me a strong sense of identification with a transsexual child I saw on television. Jack, a biological boy who had always liked to dress as a girl, told her mother that she *was* a girl, shortly after her tenth birthday. Not surprisingly, she wanted to be called Jackie. For me, the coincidence was dizzying. I had discovered another Jackie (Jackie Evancho) through my female ego state Annie, whom I had already identified as the ten-year-old girl who part of me wishes I had been. Some mental health professionals think that social transition should take place as young as possible, and some children have been treated with hormone blockers so that they will not develop as boys. A young trans girl named Jazz has attracted a lot of publicity and become an appealing and articulate spokesperson for trans children. Indeed, such children are becoming a major focus in media coverage of transgenderism.

I have had a strong emotional reaction to learning about these young trans children who are given the opportunity that I never had, although I do not know whether I would have taken it. Nor do I wish I had done so, but I still somehow wish I had had the opportunity. I read somewhere that the youngest person to have had physical transition was sixteen at the time. When she was ten, she had been very afraid of puberty and the changes that it would bring, such as a deeper voice. That age of ten keeps popping up! Since it is the age of both Annie and Chip, her trans counterpart, these stories have a heightened impact for me.

Although I basically present as male, there is one place where I can present as female and not appear male at all. That place is the Internet, where no one sees you and your words alone determine how you are perceived. I discovered that when I was first grappling with my gender identity. That was when AOL had all the chat rooms, and for a while I was using the screen name "Shaddoa," which I thought of as a version of "shadow." As a shadow, I could slip around from room to room being male, female, or genderless whenever and wherever I wanted.

I have not been in a chat room for a long time, but I still use a female name and let myself be perceived as female on a number of websites. It is like a dream world where no one questions my gender identity. It has occurred to me that I might be able to do something similar on the telephone. I do not know whether I could really sound like a woman, but I am able to speak in a reasonably high voice, especially if I use a falsetto. I have never tried it, and about the only context in which I can imagine trying it would be placing a telephone order for something. And now I always do that on the Internet.

Outside of the Internet, I never make any attempt to "pass as a woman." But in the trans community at large, "passing" is something of a holy grail—something to be sought after but very difficult to actually achieve, especially for MtFs (male-to-female transsexuals). Complete success may require very detailed plastic surgery to deal with pesky little things like an Adam's apple (sometimes a sure giveaway) and brow line. FtMs have an advantage, partly because testosterone injections enable them to grow beards, one of the most powerful of all gender indicators. Testosterone also makes the voice deeper without any special training or surgery. Nevertheless, medical transition is a huge undertaking for anyone. I have great respect for people who take that path and consider myself lucky that I was able to be successfully treated for gender dysphoria through psychotherapy alone.

Although I make no attempt to pass as a woman, the way I see it is that I pass every day. As a *man.* I am a woman incognito, masquerading, in a sense, as something I am not. Sometimes it feels almost like a role in a play. I know that when I was young, I thought it would be fun to go around unrecognized, like a spy on a secret mission. Maybe it is a bit immature of me to still think it's sort of cool, but it works for me.

Although I may masquerade as a man, I am acutely aware that I am not one. At the same time, fifty years of culturization as a man do not just evaporate. I am left with very confused feelings about the gender I rejected because it did not fit. It is still lingering around in my mind, and it influences my thoughts and feelings. When

I first realized that I am a woman, I wanted nothing to do with the attributes that I stereotypically attributed to men. I thought I understood them all too well: they were aggressive and boring. I have come to realize that many men are neither of the above.

But I am left with several important questions. How aggressive can I be as a woman? Can I identify as a woman without viewing men as enemies? And an especially big question for me: does having a man's body determine what type of woman I have to be? How masculine or feminine should I be? How strong a grip do my old stereotypes still have on me? I am still struggling to figure all of this out and to do so while living with my female gender and my male anatomy. I am still very much a work in progress, and that is why my journey is still exciting. I would not have it any other way.

Since I go incognito, I constantly have to decide where to draw the line between masculine and feminine. In general, I draw it between how I choose to appear in public and the greater freedom I allow myself in private or among people who know my secret. For example, I like jewelry. I have all sorts of necklaces and rings and a whole collection of bangles. But I am selective about what I wear where.

I will wear most of my rings both in public and in private, because I avoid flashy ones. Several of my necklaces are gold chains with or without anything hanging. Most of the others consist of some interesting ornament hanging from a black cord. Most of them I would wear some places but not others. As for my bangles, I have all sorts and will wear most of them in public, but with some discretion as to when and where. I wore a gold link bracelet somewhere and a woman we know well said she liked it because it was so masculine! Not exactly what I waned to hear, but I would not have wanted it to look too feminine, either. Always a fine line.

With some things, the line I draw is not fine. I usually carry a leather shoulder bag that functions as a purse, though I only call it that around a few people. It is dark in color and has no feminine-looking ornamentation. Also, it is taller than it is wide. I have noticed that most clearly feminine purses are designed to be more horizontal than vertical. So I stick to vertical. I do not often wear women's clothes, and when I do it is only at home and my taste runs fairly feminine. At the same time, however, I have been trying to wear more interesting men's clothes. That is an area where most men really are boring. In my attempt to liven up my vestments I have, for one thing, begun to indulge my preference for pink.

Transsexual. Lesbian. Jewelry. Clothes. Those parts of my life as a woman incognito are going well. Even things like having to use the men's room or check off "male" on one form or another are just annoyances. But something that remains unaccomplished is my quest for mindfulness. Awareness. Living in the now. There are several terms for it, but by any name it remains perhaps my most important and elusive goal. What I have in its place is a mind that, as Yoda expressed it to Luke Skywalker in *Star Wars,* is on everything except what I am doing.

Something I do or see or remember will start up a string of associations that can take my mind to any time or place in the world. Actually, the time tends to be in the past. I waste time and energy reliving things that happened long ago and obsessing over what I *should* have said or done in one situation or another. That has been going on all my life, but I am not willing to accept that it will continue for the *rest* of my life. I cannot imagine what would have as great a positive effect for me during my remaining years as becoming truly mindful. I am trying in every way I can think of to achieve that.

One way that I keep trying to be mindful is to find some "magic bullet" that will cause a breakthrough or "quantum leap" in mindfulness. Of course part of me retorts that there is no such thing, that progress toward such an important goal can only be achieved through a gradual, step-by-step process. But another part remembers times when I *did* achieve something major in what seemed like a quantum leap. A prime example is the way I stopped drinking more than thirty years ago. I had tried to quit or at least cut back on it many times before, but I would always slip back into serious drinking. Until one night when I felt that I might never take another drink, and I didn't. I was ready to stop, and I did. So now I think it is possible that sometime I will suddenly be ready for mindfulness.

I believe that keeping my mind from wandering may be easier if I have something to put in place of all the random thoughts that draw me away from what I am doing. For this purpose I have tried out several "mantras." I came up with one of the first when I was about to go to my first Philadelphia Transgender Health Conference. I was feeling a pretty severe pain my tongue and thought it was a canker sore. I wanted to see my dentist about it, but if I went to the conference, I could not see him until I got back.

Did I want to go badly enough to endure the pain for the next few days? I decided I did. I could barely stand to eat and even talking hurt, but I got through it by repeating, "hope, determination, survival" in my mind over and over again. I did survive, and when I finally got to the dentist, he found that a chip of bone or enamel from a difficult extraction had become embedded in the inside of my jaw. He managed to remove it, and I began to heal almost immediately. I will use those words again if I have to face a comparable ordeal, even though they have not enabled me to overcome the mind-wandering problem.

I have experimented with a number of other mantras, and some have been helpful, though so far nothing has brought about a quantum leap. One of my favorites is "all together," calling all of my ego states to join together so that I can act and feel like a whole person. I have also tried the single word "goddess," in an attempt to achieve conscious contact with Her. (More about the goddess in the next chapter.) Other mantras have been "love," "peace," and "dare to be aware." I take particular pleasure in using "mutant and proud," Mystique's great line in *X-men: First Class*. In fact, my main mantra at present is, "I will use my mutant power of mindfulness for good." Each of the X-Men has a particular "mutant power," and after seeing the movie I tried to figure out what mine could be.

I knew I could not shape-shift to look like anything I want nor shoot fire out of my fingertips, but I decided that true mindfulness would prove to be a very strong power. When my daughter gave me a birthday card showing Wonder Woman saying that each person has a

special power that can be used for good, I knew I was
onto something. Especially since inside the card she
wrote, "Remember to use your power for good." That
kind of acceptance and encouragement from one's
daughter would be beautiful music to any transsexual's
ears.

Even as a woman incognito, I have developed a circle of people who do know who and what I really am.
This is very important to me. The ones who live in my
own town are all members of my church. I came out to
a small group that Sue and I belonged to a few years ago
and with them I enjoyed a greater comfort level than
with other people. I once told my secret to a larger group
at church, but in all cases I was speaking in confidence.
Realistically, however, I know that it takes only one person who breaks confidence to get something into a
rumor mill, and from there it can spread like wildfire.
So for all I know, half the church may know about me
by now. But before I told any of them, I asked myself if
I would really care if the whole church found out. I did
not, and I do not.

There are some places where I do not hesitate to let
everyone know that I am a transsexual lesbian and proud
of it. Those places are explicitly for LGBT people and
their straight allies. (LGBT is the widely used shorthand
for lesbian, gay, bisexual, and transgender.) The ones
where I feel most at home have a religious or spiritual
focus. For many years I have been closely involved with
the Reconciling Ministries Network and the Church
Within a Church Movement. Both of these are organizations of United Methodists who want to change the
anti-gay beliefs and policies of our denomination.

RMN is devoted to changing the United Methodist Church from within, while CWACM is creating a model of a fully inclusive church that could be the pattern for either the UMC itself or a new denomination. With both of these groups, I have the wonderful, relaxed feeling of being with "my people." With them I know that I can be myself. I have run into many other people in these organizations at various events all over the country, and when we are together the sense of community is palpable. The opportunity to be a woman "cognito" at those times is an essential part of my comfort in being incognito the rest of the time. The fact that I do not have to censor what I say with those people does make me feel that I am living a double life, but it seems to work for me.

Another place I can be myself is at transgender conferences. Each year there are several of these in different parts of the country. The biggest, and in some ways probably the best, is the Philadelphia Trans Health Conference. It draws people of every known gender and probably a few unknown ones in an awe-inspiring display of diversity. There is a strong spiritual element for those who want it and a marvelous variety of workshops, resource booths and other events for everyone. This of course includes the focus on the extremely important issue of healthcare for trans people, whose medical needs are all too often quite poorly met.

The Trans Health Conference has a more down-to-business atmosphere than some of the others, which have a more social orientation. One of the purposes of some is to provide a safe place for crossdressers to dress as they choose, and an important offering is usually a

gala dinner dance where one can see more feminine fin-
ery than at many cisgender functions. But whatever their
specific focus, transgender conferences allow us all to
have it our way.

My involvement with the United Methodist Church
is by no means limited to my desire to change its anti-
gay characteristics. For the present, at least, it is my
church, and whatever problems I may have with some
of the rules made at the national level, I care very much
about my own congregation, and Sue and I have made
wonderful friends there. We are also quite active in it.
For Sue, her strongest spiritual connection is music, and
our local church has an excellent program under the
leadership of a music director whose talent is matched
only by her commitment. The choir is good, and Sue is,
if I say so myself, one of the best things bout it.

We both have various leadership roles in our church.
I chair the investment committee for the endowment
fund, a challenging job at a time when most mainline
Protestant churches are under severe financial pressures.
Sue faces similar issues as church treasurer, and we both
serve on the finance committee. We are also both on the
church council, which bears the administrative respon-
sibilities. Although Sue in particular also does a lot for
the church on her own, we do often act as a team. I have
been a lay member of the annual conference (which is
roughly the equivalent of a Catholic diocese) for several
years, and now Sue is, too.

United Methodist annual conferences have served
as testing grounds for the denomination's stand on
homosexuality, and ours is no exception. Year after year,
the progressive faction has introduced liberal resolutions

on the topic, but most have been voted down. Until 2015. This time, to my own surprise, the conference passed six different resolutions that challenge the denomination's discriminatory positions and practices regarding lesbian, gay, bisexual, and transgender people. Two of these are stated positions taken by our own conference, including an extremely significant statement that we will support any of our ministers who perform same-sex marriages. The other four are changes in the Book of Discipline that we will propose to the 2016 General Conference. It will be interesting to see what happens there, but I am not optimistic.

Things did not go very well at the 2012 General Conference, which meets only once every four years and has the ultimate authority in the United Methodist Church. No real progress was made on the treatment of gays in the denomination. In spite of the well-organized efforts by an impressive coalition of progressive groups, the conservatives maintained a firm grip on what legislation was passed. The United Methodist Church is deeply divided, and I have no idea what the short-term developments will be. But in the long term, we who desire full inclusion will prevail. History is on our side.

The young people in our denomination and others are blazing a new trail. The only question is how long it will take, and the problem is that in the meantime a lot of people are being hurt by their own religion.

Religion should help people, not hurt them. But many in the transgender community have felt its sting much more than its blessing. During my remaining years, I would like to show that it does not have to be that way. But am I up to the task? The truth is that success has always been very elusive for me. Even when I have come close to it, I have always seemed to find a way to sabotage myself. I have been a master at snatching defeat from the jaws of victory. I have always given up on things only to discover later how well it would have worked out if I had stuck with them. Never thinking that I have time to finish anything. Starting so many things and bringing so few to completion. Can it be any different this time? I have to believe that it can. Maybe that belief has been the missing ingredient.

CHAPTER XII

TRANSCENDER LEE

If the past is prologue, then everything that has happened during my journey up until now is the launching pad for whatever comes next. One constant theme so far, both on my path to self-discovery and on my path since then as a self-identified woman, has been my attraction to religion and spirituality. Even when I wanted nothing to do with religion, I could never stay away from it. My need for a spiritual component in my life had to be satisfied, one way or another.

During the search I tried out Catholicism, Episcopalianism, Methodism, the Quakers, and the Baptists. I was also intrigued by various versions of both Eastern and Western mysticism. My active participation in religious institutions began as an altar boy and now includes service to the United Methodist Church at both the local church and the annual conference levels. And although I like much about that denomination and am working to change some things I do not like about it, I now feel the need for a religious and spiritual life that extends beyond any one religion.

In addition to searching for a faith tradition I could identify with, during certain stages of my life I have also wanted to be a minister of one sort or another. When I was about to graduate from high school, I thought I was going to become a Jesuit priest. Although that did not happen, only about six months later I dropped out of college intending to join a Trappist monastery. I did not do that, either. Later in college, during my Baptist period, the thought of being a Protestant minister attracted me. Still later, it was the Episcopalian priesthood. Now I once again feel called to ministry but, as with my present spiritual outlook in general, I find myself looking beyond the parameters of any one-faith tradition.

The point of starting a ministry now would be to expand upon what I am trying to do with this book. The primary message of *Woman Incognito* is that the options for some people whose gender identity does not match their assigned sex may include non-transition. They may not need to change their bodies to match their true gender. If they suffer from gender dysphoria, they may discover, as I did, that with the help of therapy they can be happy simply remaining women in male bodies or men in female bodies. My hope is that this message may not only help people struggling with their own gender issues to decide how to deal with them but also help all trans people, as well as the general public, to better understand the full scope of the gender spectrum.

As I thought about the word "trans," it occurred to me that what trans people do is to "transcend" the boundaries of gender. Then I remembered a lesson I had learned several years ago from three amazing leaders in the cause of justice. They taught me that justice is indivisible and that we cannot achieve it for some without seeking it for all. So I decided that although my ministry could focus particularly on transcending boundaries of gender, it would also need to address boundaries of race, religion, class, and sexual orientation.

Shortly before the 2013 Philadelphia Trans Health Conference, I had begun to think about my gender identity and my present approach to spirituality in a way I had never thought of before, and I had a chance to explain my idea in one of the workshops. The presenter asked us whether we thought our spirituality had any connection with being transsexual. I responded that for me the interfaith spiritual perspective that I have been developing recently seems somewhat parallel to my gender identity and that the two appear to go together both logically and emotionally. Just as I have come to see gender as a spectrum containing many different variations, all equally legitimate, I have also come to think of spirituality as a spectrum containing many different faith traditions, all equally valid. The processes by which my views on gender and spirituality have evolved to their present state also seem parallel.

I grew up with a very simple view of gender. Boys had penises and girls had vaginas. End of story. Boys and men were called males and girls and women were called females. Males thought, felt, and acted in ways that were called masculine. Females thought, felt, and acted in ways that were called feminine. Boys loved girls; girls loved boys. And you could tell all those things about people just from what was between their legs. Except that it did not always work out that way.

Some boys did not seem all that masculine, and some girls did not seem all that feminine. It turned out that some girls liked toy trucks more than dolls and some boys wanted ballet lessons rather than football practice.

And by the time I was a teenager, I realized that what was supposed to be a prime law of nature, as dependable as the law of gravity, was not always followed. Some boys were actually attracted to other boys, not to girls. Some girls were attracted to girls, not to boys. What was that about?

It got even more complicated when I was college age. I discovered that a biological male could even *feel* like a woman. Even think he *was* a woman. I thought that *I* might really be a woman. But it took another few decades for me to understand that I really am a woman even though I have a male body, and that as such I am simply part of a broad gender spectrum that encompasses not only a whole continuum from male to female but even some identities that lie outside that continuum.

The evolution of my spiritual understanding has followed a similar path. Being raised as a Catholic, I started out with the certainty that Catholicism was the one true religion. End of story. But at some point I started thinking, why just Catholicism? Why not all of Christianity? And eventually, why just Christianity? Why not accept all religions as equally valid? Finally, why assume that spirituality is confined to those traditions that are generally considered to be religions? Do not other systems of values, beliefs, and practices also fall under the broad umbrella of spirituality? And what about artistic or scientific creativity? At this point in my own spiritual journey, I am prepared to accept that they all do.

Does the similarity between the way I reached an awareness of being transsexual and the way I developed my present interfaith approach to spirituality mean that this is the "correct" form of spirituality for transsexuals?

I would certainly not say that, although it does work for me. Still, for several years I have been interested in whether there is such a thing as a distinctively transgender spirituality or theology. At the Trans Health Conference I had the opportunity both to express my views and to hear other transgender people discuss their own spirituality. I came away with the sense that most of them do not really think there is a uniquely transgender spirituality, but believe that each trans person has to develop his or her own spiritual path. I still wonder whether there could be some particular spiritual style or approach that would be distinctively transgender. Alternatively, there might be some common element in the spirituality of transgender people that is directly related to being transgender, even if in other ways their individual forms of spirituality might be very diverse. I am sure that I will continue to ponder these questions and seek the opinions of other trans people.

Whether or not anyone's spirituality is specifically transsexual, I intend to develop a ministry that transcends gender, as well as race, religion, class, and sexual orientation. But what preparation do I have for such an undertaking? I believe that my whole life so far has prepared me for this particular ministry. That includes but is not limited to my entire education (both formal and informal) and my varied religious experiences.

Although I am aware of some gaps in my background, I think I can make up for them. I am also mindful of the expression, "If not you, who? And if not now, when?" As for the who part, I feel that my combination of relevant experience and facility with both written and oral communication makes me the right person, ready

or not. And as for the when part, I think that the very
great increase of both knowledge and understanding
about transgenderism in recent years has made this the
right time to expand people's awareness of the full
breadth and implications of the gender spectrum.

Even though I see my whole life as preparation for
a transcending interfaith ministry focusing on transgender issues, I will have to gain some more specialized education, especially on the interfaith side. Like most people
whose religious base has been Christianity, I have had
precious little exposure to other religions. I suppose the
same holds true for most people who come from other
faith traditions, but I am especially aware of the "one
true religion" message of my own religion. I have moved
away from that attitude, but now I have to put some specific knowledge behind my interfaith theory. The big
question is, how to go about it?

The traditional path to learning how to be a minister is to attend a seminary of some sort. Most of them
are dedicated to some specific religion or even a specific
branch of a religion, as in the case of denomination-affil-
iated seminaries within Christianity. The idea of a truly
interfaith seminary seems quite recent, with the New
Seminary in New York (now over thirty years old) apparently being a pioneer in the field. There are a few others
with actual physical locations and a number that operate
entirely on the Internet. Although I have no problem
with the concept of distance learning via the Internet,
such institutions are widely regarded as just "diploma
mills." A number of them clearly deserve that reputation,
but a few may not. Unfortunately, especially when
degrees are granted, perception is the crucial factor in

whether the institution and its degrees will be respected or serve any practical purpose. And that brings up the whole issue of degrees.

There are all sorts of graduate level degrees in the field of religion. Some have a strictly academic focus, like a master's or doctorate in theology, while others are essentially professional degrees for ministers, like the Master or Divinity or Doctor of Ministry. The big question about any degree is whether it is from an accredited institution. There are many so-called accrediting organizations, but the problem is, who accredits the accreditors? In the United States the general answer is the government, although accreditation by various professional organizations is also highly respected. For seminaries this means the Association of Theological Schools, but its member schools are all Christian.

I would personally be very hesitant about getting a degree from any school that is not accredited, although if one seemed to have standards comparable to those of accredited schools it might be interesting to get a degree and be prepared to document the legitimacy of the program. Another possibility I might consider would be some religious or philosophical degree not offered by accredited schools. That way it could not be accused of not meeting the same standards. Once again, I would want to be prepared to document why it deserves respect. Most of the respected interfaith seminaries seem to avoid the whole accreditation issue by just not granting degrees. Their only claim is that they train people for interfaith ministry according to their own standards, which they openly discuss. Their programs lead not to a degree but to ordination.

There is, of course, a way to sidestep the whole issue
of degrees, accreditation, choice of online or residential
school, and so forth: just do it yourself. There have
always been people who have learned as much as they
want about any field or fields without schools and even
without teachers. How do they do it? Traditionally, there
have been four basic methods: learning by doing, seeing,
reading, and listening. These methods have been used
for thousands of years, and they are still the ways to learn
on your own. But the twentieth and twenty-first centuries have brought new technology that has greatly
enhanced our ability to use these time-honored methods
of learning.

First came radio, recording, motion pictures, and
television. Their impact was tremendous. They brought
distant parts of the world closer together and made
knowledge much more readily available than in earlier
centuries. They paved the way for the information explo-
sion launched by the digital age and the Internet. The
latter has created the biggest library the world has ever
known and made incredible amounts of information
from all over the world available to us almost instanta-
neously. There has never been such a great time for the
autodidact (self-educator).

Now we can have virtual experiences that were previously accessible to very few people and see almost anything from almost anywhere. We can hear the voices and
sounds of people and things everywhere. We can read
books, periodicals, and documents of every sort, wherever the originals are located. And it all happens at the
stroke of a key. If I take this route to continue preparation for my ministry, I will be able to design my own

program of study as I go along, adding and subtracting things as the spirit moves. The idea is very appealing.

It occurs to me that I could even share the process of educating myself for interfaith ministry. I could use a blog or some other Internet medium to explain my goals and plans and journal my progress. It could be an interesting view of the development of an educational program while it is actually taking place. I could invite others to develop their own self-education programs, and if they gained any inspiration from mine, so much the better. For me, the process will never end. But at some point I might decide that I had done enough for a basic program of education for interfaith ministry. Then I might codify what I have done and publish it as a model that anyone could follow, modifying it as much as seems appropriate for his or her own purpose. And by writing this paragraph, I myself have come up with a project that could actually be a part of my own interfaith ministry.

However I deal with the preparation for ministry issue, there is still the question of ordination. Most people believe that a minister has to have been ordained, although there has also been a tradition in some branches of Christianity that it is only necessary to have "heard the call." Saint Paul did not claim that he had been ordained by any human authority. He just said that he had been called to be an apostle. I heard my favorite example of this concept one time when the legendary prizefighter Muhammad Ali was being interviewed on television. He was referring to himself as a Muslim minister, but the interviewer said that you have to be made a minister by some "recognized authority." Ali replied, "Allah is recognized." One more knockout punch by the champ. Nevertheless, I have been struggling with the issue of how and whether to be ordained.

The Church Within a Church Movement has performed ordinations for several candidates who had gone through the seminary training of the United Methodist Church, but who for one reason or another were denied ordination by that denomination. At the one held in Tucson in 2011, there was much talk of defining oneself rather than accepting definitions imposed by one's society or culture. So why, I found myself wondering, should I accept other people's definitions of "church" or "minister" or "ordination"? Why should I not decide that an Internet church is as much a church as any other, and that ordination by such a church is as valid as any other? After all, CWACM conducts its ordinations on its own authority, not anyone else's.

Of course, I have not had the formal training that the CWACM ordinands have had, but why must I let others define what is appropriate training for a minister? Why should I not decide that my own education and experience constitute appropriate preparation for my particular ministry and that the only recognition my calling requires is from God? At this point in my life, I do not have the years that it takes to prepare for ordination in the Methodist tradition or that of many other Christian denominations. And even if I did, the focused emphasis on a single-faith tradition would probably not be the best use of those years if my goal is an interfaith ministry.

Where does that leave me? I tried to figure out what my alternatives are. One was an Internet ordination. There are scads of Internet churches ready to hand out ordinations. The usual pitch is that you will have the legal right to perform marriages. What they do not always tell you is that their ordinations are not accepted in all states. Putting the wedding issue aside, most of the online ordinations are available to anyone, even just as a joke. There are stories of people getting their pets ordained. Some online ordinations are handled entirely by computer with no humans involved.

There are a few seemingly serious Internet churches, and some of these have an interfaith orientation. I joined one of them and got ordained. They at least make an effort to ordain only real people, though they acknowledge that some may do it only as a novelty. They have a LISTSERV by which their ministers can communicate with each other, and it became obvious that some of them take it very seriously. For a while I took that ordination seriously, but at this time I do not think I would use it to claim to be an ordained minister. The general perception that Internet ordinations are phony just seems too strong for me to challenge. So I started to look for a traditional church willing to ordain me.

I finally found a Baptist church that would do so on the basis of my call to ministry by God, my considerable though not primarily religious education, and my experience in various churches and religious organizations. The Baptist tradition is that their churches are completely autonomous, so each one can establish its own criteria for ordination. I have received their ordination and consider it valid, though I am not sure how much use I will make of it. This is partly because I am currently questioning whether I need any ordination at all, or whether I would do best just to establish a lay ministry and leave it at that. I could call myself a minister, lay minister, unordained minister, or something else entirely.

If I have a ministry, I suppose that would make me a minister, ordained or not. Would that satisfy my life-long, though intermittent, desire to be a minister? Maybe, but there still might be a problem. Would being a lay minister or unordained minister entitle me to use the title "Reverend"? And why would that matter? Two possible reasons. First, I just think that title, whether spoken or printed, immediately indicates that its bearer performs some sort of religious function.

The second and more personal reason is that I like the idea of a gender-neutral title. I feel quite strongly that for me "Mr." is a masquerade, and "Miss," "Mrs.," or "Ms." would be confusing, misleading, or both. That is one reason why I wanted a doctorate, since "Doctor" is also gender neutral. But apparently that was not enough to motivate me through a dissertation, so "Reverend" has seemed like my best bet. For quite some time, I was in fact thinking of myself as Reverend Lee.

Ironically, at first I was thinking of Reverend Lee as male. I guess old stereotypes die hard. I had grown up when almost all ministers, and of course all Catholic priests, were men. I still had that image in my mind, even though for many years I have championed the idea of women in those roles. I once even used a male pronoun when referring to Reverend Lee with my therapist. She pointed out what I had said, and then I started deliberately thinking of Reverend Lee as female. She is, after all, simply myself in a professional role. Which of course raises the question, just what will that role be?

Only time will tell. There are many possible directions my proposed ministry may take. The first major step is finishing this book. It will be the core of the ministry, whatever else it may include. My target audience for *Woman Incognito* comprises three groups: people currently struggling with their gender issues, the rest of the trans community, and the general public. For each group, the context is helping people understand the full range of possibilities within the gender spectrum. But I want my ministry to address more than just gender issues. I want it to transcend boundaries not only of gender but also of race, religion, class, and sexual orientation. I have come to realize that justice for any group of people is ultimately intertwined with justice for all groups. This concept is sometimes called the "intersection of oppressions."

My ministry will be both transcending and interfaith. Therefore it will by its nature attempt to move across religious boundaries, which have done so much to divide people and thwart efforts to achieve peace and understanding. Race is obviously still a huge justice issue throughout the world, and attitudes about both gender identity and sexual orientation seem to differ among various races and ethnicities. As I write this, it was only two days ago that same-sex marriage became legal in my own state, placing it squarely within the growing movement for full civil rights for gays and lesbians. But there is still serious prejudice and discrimination against them. Since so many trans people are gay in their true genders, it is especially important for a trans-focused ministry to include gay equality among its goals. And then there is class.

Coming from a somewhat affluent and highly educated family, I am now acutely aware of many things that I always took for granted because I was in a privileged class. When I was young, I was always hearing that Americans, unlike the British, were not separated into different classes. I am not sure how long I believed that, but I now realize that boundaries of class need to be transcended just as much as those of other types of segregation and categorization that divide and oppress people.

So much for ambitious goals. They are certainly important, but what will I actually *do*, beyond writing this book? The easy answer would be that after starting out with the book, I will simply go wherever the path leads. That would be true, but I have already done some thinking about possible components of the ministry. If this book receives attention in the trans community, I will very likely conduct some workshops at trans conferences and may be invited to speak at some trans events. If it receives attention outside that community, I might be able to reach a broader audience in a similar way.

And then there is the Internet. That strikes me as the premiere venue for religion and spiritual activity in the twenty-first century. It will not replace physical houses of worship, but it will make it possible for people all across the country and all around the world to come together in the same virtual venue. And it seems especially appropriate for an interfaith ministry that is trying to honor all spiritual traditions and all peoples.

The ways that the Internet can be used are countless. For starters we would almost certainly have a website with a number of different pages for different aspects of the ministry. There would be material about gender and material about the interfaith approach to spirituality. Race, class, and sexual orientation could be explored either separately or together. And of course there would be links to other sites relevant to each topic addressed in our site. There could be papers and articles and ways to make the site interactive, like forums and even chat rooms. We would probably have a blog. And we would not have to be limited to text and graphics. We could have music and streaming audio and videos on You Tube. Is all this outlandishly ambitious? Maybe. The point is that we could start out as small as we want and grow in whatever directions we want to and are able to.

Although our ministry will be interfaith, as individuals each of us will have our own form of spiritual energy and our own ideas of the God who is worshipped under so many different names. Since our basic interfaith perspective is that all paths to God are equally valid, none of us will claim that whatever path we take is the "true" path, but simply the one that works for us. My slogan is, "Many paths, one destination." That destination is God, because there is no place else to go.

So what is our concept of God? What is our theology? There is no right answer. We can accept the theology of the faith tradition we were raised in or that any of the other religions in the world, confident that it is as valid as any. Or we can develop our own. That is what I am doing, and I would encourage others to try it. You can put together your own ideas and whatever elements from existing religions have meaning for you. I know I used to hear that you had to accept your religion and its scriptures and teachings whole. You could not just choose the parts you liked and ignore the rest. But why not? Why should we expect one size to fit all? To me the point of a theology is that it works for you, giving your spiritual life a cohesive context.

Your personal theology need not replace that of your own tradition or current religion, because both will be equally valid. I do not expect the process of developing my own personal theology to end until my consciousness reaches the ultimate level of full union with God. Perhaps some day I will publish my personal theology, both to express my thoughts and to provide others with an example of what one might look like. But for now I will describe only a few parts of it, chosen because of how they relate to basic themes in this book.

A question that would seem relevant to most transgender people is what gender is God? Is God male or female? Or neither? Or both? Or some other gender altogether? Is God whatever gender a person is most comfortable with? I used to strongly oppose the traditional assumption that God is male and vigorously advocate for gender-inclusive language. But when I discovered my own womanhood, I found myself thinking of God as female. I felt best able to relate to God as the goddess. But then it occurred to me that if it was all right for me to think of her as female because that worked best for me, it should also be acceptable for others to think of God as male. As masculine. As father. For myself. I think in terms of a single goddess, manifested as all the traditional goddesses and also some not always thought of that way, such as Mary Magdalene and Joan of Arc.

Even if we should all be free to think of God as the gender we can best relate to, there remains a question that is currently being asked a lot. What about scripture and traditional religious music? Should it be rewritten so as to use only gender-inclusive language, never calling the deity anything like father or applying gender-specific pronouns to said deity?

In regard to scripture, I think gender should always stay true to the original. We do not have to like the author's terminology, but we should not change what he or she said just because it does not match our own preference. In general I would say the same about the words in hymns and other religious music, but words to other types of music are frequently rewritten, and I do not feel as strongly about that as I do about scriptures. When it comes to old songs, that is. But when it comes to new songs, I would go back to the idea of using whatever words the writer is most comfortable with (or thinks the intended audience would be most comfortable with).

If God's gender relates to the transgender focus of my proposed ministry, the next question relates to its interfaith character. Just what does it mean to say that many paths lead to a single destination, which is the goddess? In my personal theology, we are all parts of her, and our common destination consists of complete consciousness of our own divinity. Since I think that everyone will eventually reach this level of consciousness, my theology is Universalist. In a Christian context, that means that all are saved. In my personal theology, being saved would equate to transcending everything that deters us from complete consciousness of our own divinity. In this as in everything, my personal theology does not repudiate my Christian tradition but expands my understanding of spirituality in a way that works best for me.

So the question remains, how can I best share the things I have learned and experienced in a way that will benefit others who are facing similar issues? I have been working on this chapter for quite a while, and my thoughts and plans have kept evolving. I have said a lot about the "ministry" I am planning, but what form do I want it to take? I cannot help thinking of calling it a church. An Internet church, to be exact, in spite of the bad reputation Internet churches seem to have. And, in a way, *because* of that, I believe it is unfortunate that they are not being taken seriously. Think about it. This is the twenty-first century, and a whole new generation has grown up with the Internet. They spend a huge part of their lives there. That is where they meet with their friends, make new friends, do their schoolwork, play games, listen to music, watch movies, and do almost everything else.

The Internet is the *natural* venue for the twenty-first-century church. The big churches and mainline denominations are figuring that out. They are launching online ministries all over the place, which I think is great. But churches that exist *only* on the Internet are still being regarded with great suspicion. Why? I think it is largely the fault of many of the Internet churches themselves. They have marketed themselves primarily as ordination mills. They advertise all over the Internet with the promise of making you a "legally ordained minister" immediately. And why should you want that? The biggest reason, touted on website after website, is so that you can conduct marriages. In some states that works, and the wedding can be as religious or nonreligious as the officiant and the couple want it to be. But the role actually played by the Internet church in such cases is more about law than religion.

The public does not regard ordinations from those churches as "real" and does not regard the churches that hand them out as real, either. Some of the churches seem more commercial than religious. Although they usually make a point of not charging for the ordination itself, they often have a whole store full of fancy certificates of ordination, credentials, and numerous types of ministerial supplies. Another aspect of most of these churches that makes them look suspicious is that they usually seem to have *only* ministers and no ordinary members. Many also offer online education for their ministers, often conferring degrees that require far less work than a comparable degree from any accredited institution.

Most of the churches I have been discussing could almost be used as textbooks on how *not* to design an Internet church, which is part of why I am tempted to try to show how to do it right. For one thing, I would not focus on ordaining people. I would try to offer things that would make people want to be part of an online congregation. If ordination ever were offered, it would not be handed out just for the asking. There would have to be some documentation of education (formal or informal), religious background and experience, and reasons for wanting to be ordained. An applicant would have to make a convincing demonstration of sincerity. At least one face-to-face meeting could be required.

While the process might be simpler and less time-consuming than a traditional seminary program, it would not be quick and easy. It would not be worth the effort just to satisfy a whim, get an impressive certificate to hang on the wall, or perform a couple of weddings. It would also be quite complicated and perhaps somewhat expen-

sive to administer, since real people would be evaluating
the qualifications of real people, rather than computers
simply processing data transmitted from other computers.
Even if I wanted to, I do not see how I could include ordination in the services offered by an Internet church that I
would be capable of launching. And since I do not know
of any existing Internet church that offers an ordination
that would satisfy my own criteria, I still have not
answered the question of what sort of ministerial credentials I would need in order to found and run a church.

At this point I think I would take the position either
that ordination is not necessary (and I honestly do not
see why it should be) or that I have been ordained
directly by God (which I actually believe). Even setting
aside the whole ordination issue, the attempt to show
that an Internet church could deserve to be taken seriously would be a daunting task. I fear that this would be
such a demanding goal in itself that it could distract me
from my original goal of transcending boundaries of
gender, race, religion, class, and sexual orientation. But
maybe not. Maybe it would simply be an effective vehicle for pursuing that goal. I am obviously still thinking
about it, but now I am also thinking about quite a different approach.

My latest idea is to dispense altogether with the
words "minister," "ministry," and "church." Those words
tend to be associated with Christianity, and I am on an
interfaith mission. *Mission.* That is a good word, and no
one religion can lay exclusive claim to it. If I want a formal legal entity, it could simply be a nonprofit organization, an interfaith one, which strives to transcend
boundaries. It could even be structured as a business,

which would be able to pursue the same goals and do the same things, but without certain restrictions placed on nonprofits.

What would that make me, as the founder and president of the organization? If my goal is to transcend boundaries, why not "transcender"? For some time I have been seeking an appropriate title for an interfaith religious leader, but everything I thought of turned out to be linked to some particular religion. Until I came up with this one. In reality, all religions seek to transcend the boundaries of ordinary human experience in order to achieve some higher vision of life. I want to do that in such a way as to transcend even the boundaries of religion itself. I want to be a transcender. Transcender Lee. I like the sound of that.

This book has been about a journey. It has been an exciting journey. It still is, and I hope to learn about the journeys of many of my fellow travelers in the largely uncharted territory known as gender. Only a few decades ago, very little was known about gender as distinguished from sex. The idea that a person's gender could be different from his or her sex assigned at birth was almost unknown. Most state-of-the-art mental health professionals did not even have the transsexual phenomenon on their radar screens.

A lot of progress has been made in just the last ten or fifteen years, but there is still a long, long way to go. And those of us who are currently living the transsexual experience are in the vanguard of the gender journey into the future. Let us move onward together, transcending boundaries of gender and whatever else threatens to confine us in restrictive categories.

CHAPTER XIII

THINGS I WISH MY PARENTS HAD KNOWN

I have told my story so far and I have shared my thoughts about where it may go from here. But there are countless transsexuals across the country and around the world whose stories are just beginning or who are just now discovering that their stories are transsexual stories. The form their stories take will be shaped substantially by their parents' reactions. I myself wonder at times how different my life might have been had my parents understood more about the transsexual experience. Of course I will never know, and the amount *anyone* understood about gender at that time was severely limited. But things have changed dramatically since my youth.

This is, in fact, a great time to be parenting a transsexual child. In recent years there has been a quantum leap in knowledge and awareness about gender among both mental health professionals and the general public. The transsexual phenomenon has been explored in movies, on television, in magazines and newspapers, and all over the Internet. The purpose of this chapter is simply to help parents get started on the challenging and exciting experience of raising children who are part of a major shift in our society's gender paradigm.

When I was growing up, the gender paradigm was simple. Gender was the same as sex and everyone was either male or female. It is now understood that gender is not something physical, like sex organs, but rather a person's inner feeling of being male or female or even something else. There are many people who self-identify as the gender opposite the sex they were assigned at birth, which was based on their anatomy. Such people are called transsexuals. Sometimes they are called transgender instead, but that is actually a broader term that includes people who do not think of themselves as either male or female or simply do not fit the traditional expectations for either gender.

This chapter is specifically for parents of transsexuals, although in the early stages of trying to determine whether a child is transsexual, it is important to understand that not all children who exhibit some characteristic of the other sex are actually transsexual. Some may be transgender in some other way. But if your child *is* transsexual, some good news has been coming from the mental health professionals recently. The trend is to no longer consider being transsexual a mental disorder.

The new understanding is that a transsexual has a mental disorder only if the mismatch between gender and physical sex causes distress or discomfort, as it often does. In those cases, the distress or discomfort is known as gender dysphoria. It is the dysphoria that requires treatment, not the simple fact of being transsexual. And although physical transition used to be considered the only effective treatment for transsexuals, the professionals are also starting to realize that in some cases the gender dysphoria can be treated by psychotherapy alone.

There is another thing that parents need to be aware of. Being transsexual has nothing to do with sexual orientation. Transsexuals can be either straight or gay. They seem to tend to be attracted to the same sex as before they knew they were transsexual. A male to female transsexual (MtF or "trans woman") who liked women and seemed to be straight will very likely turn out to be a gay woman, and one who seemed to be a gay man will very likely turn out to be a straight woman. The same is true for female to male transsexuals (FtMs or "trans men"), except the other way around. And although some gay men seem somewhat feminine and some gay women seem somewhat masculine, as long as they identify with the genders that match their biological sex, that is completely different from being transsexual.

If there are so many things that do *not* mean your child is transsexual, how are you supposed to know if he or she actually is? First of all, there is no certain answer. Young children in particular may experiment with clothes and toys and activities generally associated with the opposite sex simply as part of figuring out what gender is all about. Often parents want to think that such activities are just a "phase," and indeed they may be. The issue is further complicated by the fact that "tomboys" are considered more acceptable in our society than are "sissies." But if either a boy or a girl continues such behaviors on a regular basis for an extended period of time, you may be dealing with much more than just a phase.

The clearest sign that a child is really transsexual comes if an apparent boy explicitly says he is a girl, or an apparent girl explicitly says she is a boy. Even such a declaration might not be conclusive if it happens only for a brief period of time. But if you hear it frequently and persistently, your child is very likely expressing what he or she really feels very deeply. Expressing, in other words, his or her true gender. This is all the more likely if the feeling is accompanied by gender dysphoria. The older the child becomes, the more seriously the feeling and the dysphoria (if present) should be taken, and if they continue into the teen years you should probably assume that your child really is transsexual. But it will very likely be evident by the time of puberty.

So you are convinced that your child is or probably is transsexual. It is almost certain to hit you very hard. This is not what you expected. It seems to turn all your expectations for your child's life and even your own life upside down. Your first reaction may be to wish he or she could just be normal. You may be angry and resentful at God or the Universe or Mother Nature. Didn't nature or whatever totally get it wrong this time?

All these negative feelings are normal, and they are nothing to be ashamed of. You will feel a sense of loss, and indeed you have suffered a loss. You have lost the boy or girl you thought you had and whom you love. You will have to mourn that loss. But you have also gained something wonderful. You will come to feel the way one parent I know felt when she said, "I had an unhappy daughter and now I have a happy son. How could I feel anything but glad?" In reality, your child is the same person as before. The difference is that now you understand more about him or her than before. That is something to be grateful for.

No one yet knows what causes someone to be transsexual. But there is one thing parents can be sure of: they did not cause it. Many parents ask themselves, "What did we do wrong?" Nothing. There is nothing you did and nothing you did not do that could make your child transsexual. This can be hard to accept, but you must accept it, because to think you caused it by doing something wrong means that you think there is something wrong with your child. There isn't. To understand that and to have a positive attitude toward raising your child to be happy and healthy, it is important for you to have your own support system composed of friends, relatives, and anyone else who can help provide an affirming environment for your child.

One person you will definitely need is a mental health professional. Both you and your child have entered into territory that is sure to be somewhat bewildering, and you cannot be expected to navigate it without the help of an expert guide. Fortunately, there are now a substantial number of therapists with specialized knowledge and experience in transgender issues. A good one will not start out with any preconceived ideas about how to deal with your child's gender identity. Instead, the appropriate professional will help you and your child discover and achieve whatever solution is best for him or her.

No matter what the best direction for your child's life turns out to be, the family home environment will play a crucial role in achieving a happy outcome. What he or she needs more than anything else is your love, support, understanding, and protection. A trans woman who is beautiful, successful, and active in the movement for transgender equality has said, "I wish my parents had known how to provide an atmosphere in our family home life where I felt safe and secure to share with them the gender feeling and longing I experienced in my childhood. My earliest memories are all those of hiding and secrecy, hoping I wouldn't get caught in my mother's things. I wish I could have felt safe and secure coming to my mother to share presenting to my family rather than hiding." That pretty well sums up what trans children need from their parents in their home lives. They need total acceptance of who they really are, unconditional love, and a sense of security. They need affirming behavior such as calling them by their preferred names and referring to them by their preferred pronouns. Those two things may at first be difficult to do, but they mean a huge amount to transsexuals because they signify acceptance of their true identities.

Trans children also need help from their parents in dealing with the outside world, which may be far less supportive of them. At the present time, many people are encouraging trans children to transition socially at quite a young age. What this means is that a transsexual girl will start dressing like a girl, wearing her hair like a girl, playing with girls' toys, and everything else that is culturally associated with girls. If she is socially transitioning before puberty, she will probably hang around mostly with girls. In sum, she will "live as a girl," at least to the extent that other children and adults will let her.

In the same ways, a socially transitioning transsexual boy will live as a boy to the extent that he is allowed to. And there's the rub. There are innumerable ways that genetic boys, girls, and adults will resist accepting trans girls or boys as "real" girls or boys. Although progress is being made, our society still doesn't "get it" when anatomical males and anatomical females say they are

really female and male, respectively. And this is nowhere
more true than in the place where most children have to
be, which is school.

At school, you and your child will face a whole array
of thorny issues, both general attitudes and practical
problems. The one that *always* comes up is which bathroom a trans child should use. Sometimes schools try to
get around that one by having trans children use teachers' bathrooms. But as I write this, the courts seem to be
deciding that trans boys and girls must be allowed to use
the same bathrooms as other boys and girls. This trend,
though encouraging, is likely to bring up outrage, resentment, and fear among children, parents, teachers, and
administrators. Add to that such issues as locker rooms,
traditionally single-sex sports teams, potential bullying
and ostracism, etcetera, etcetera, and schools can become
battlefields in a culture war.

Throughout all the inevitable turmoil and controversy as schools struggle to adjust to a new gender paradigm, parents of transsexual children have to be their
prime advocates. They may have to go head-to-head
with school administrators to fight for their child's best
interests and to help negotiate viable solutions to the difficult issues facing both them and their schools. It has
been suggested that parents might do well to discuss
some of these issues with their children to learn what
they want and expect at school before confronting school
authorities. It is, after all, the comfort and safety of the
transsexual children themselves that is the objective in
all this. And rather than having new rules and policies
thrust upon the teachers without preparation, parents
could ask that training be provided to help both teachers

and staff understand and deal with issues involving gender identity.

Schools are only one context in which parents will have to learn how to advocate for their transsexual children. For some, another important area will be religion. It is a sad fact that a very high percentage of transsexuals grow up believing that religion is their enemy. And all too often they have good reason. Although my basic attitude toward religion is that all faith traditions are valid ways to seek God, I cannot support religious practices that vilify people, especially their own adherents, for characteristics that are part of their God-given identities.

Those parents who are raising their children in a specific religion should try to motivate their churches to deliver a message that respects the diversity of God's children. If their church or religion cannot do that, they may have to make the difficult choice of either looking for another one with a more positive message or, if they feel they cannot do that, trying to counteract the negative religious influence on their children's lives with their own positive message.

After your child has transitioned socially, and you have navigated the disrespect, prejudice, and discriminatory treatment found in schools, churches, and many other contexts for a while, your child may want to go farther. He or she may express a desire for medical treatments that will make his or her body more closely match his or her gender. There is an increasing belief that adolescence is the right time for physical transition, but that brings up the issue of puberty. If a teenager has hormone therapy or sex reassignment surgery (SRS), he or she will actually experience a second puberty. For that reason, some specialists are recommending hormone blockers to postpone puberty.

If the time comes when your son or daughter wants to transition physically, there are many options to consider. Hormone therapy by itself causes dramatic changes, which some people find sufficient. Beyond the physical effects, trans people on hormones tend to develop various preferences, attitudes, and behaviors generally associated with the gender opposite their biological sex. Those who want to go farther will find numerous types of SRS available. This is serious surgery, and as with all surgery, there are risks involved. But for many transsexuals, it seems to be the only way to achieve fulfillment in their true genders.

Since physical transition can be done to various degrees, terms have been developed to distinguish some of the basic approaches. Transsexuals who have had SRS are commonly known as post-operative, or "post-op." Those who have had hormone therapy and want SRS but have not yet had it are called pre-operative, or "pre-op." Someone who has had hormone therapy but does *not* want SRS is called "non-op."

So far there has really been no word for someone who self-identifies as the gender opposite the sex he or she was assigned at birth but does not want *any* physical (or even social) transition. To fill this gap in terminology, I am using the term "non-transition transsexual." I use this term for people who, like myself, are women in male bodies or men in female bodies, believe that is what they are supposed to be, and are happy to remain that way. I think it is important for parents of a trans child to understand that for some this may be a viable option. Another possibility they need to be aware of is that their child may choose to transition socially but not physically.

In this chapter I have tried to help parents understand their transsexual children by sharing with them some of the things I wish my own parents had known. But I have only scratched the surface. Fortunately, we live at a time when vast amounts of information and ideas about gender identity are readily available to anyone who is interested. Even the popular media provide a steady flow of material. Newspapers and magazines offer news related to transsexual individuals and issues on an almost daily basis. Several books tell personal stories of growing up and living transsexual, although so far this is the only one I know of by a transsexual who has chosen not to transition. Transsexual characters have been depicted in television shows and movies, whether comedies, dramas, or documentaries. My favorite such film, as mentioned previously, is *Ma Vie en Rose,* a sensitive story about a seven-year-old boy who is convinced that he was supposed to be a girl.

There are a number of high quality organizations that can help you in your effort to accept, understand, and support your transsexual child. The premier organization, in spite of its name, is Parents, Families and Friends of Lesbians and Gays (PFLAG). When it began back in the 1970s, the whole transgender issue was not on many people's radar. But it became aware of the need to expand its scope, and by the 1990s, was welcoming parents of transgender children.

Although PFLAG did not change its name, it developed a new transgender network called TNET. It published an excellent booklet called *Welcoming Our Trans*

Family and Friends, which was actually my source for some of the information and ideas in this chapter. PFLAG is a large, active organization with over 200,000 members and several hundred local chapters. I would encourage you to join and to become involved in a local group. It is a place where you can meet other parents like you who love, accept, and encourage children who do not come out of our society's typical gender mold.

Several other organizations can also give you help and valuable information. The World Professional Association for Transgender Health publishes *Standards of Care*, which is the most widely accepted guide for the treatment of patients with gender dysphoria. The National Gay and Lesbian Task Force publishes *Transgender Equality: A Handbook for Activists and Policy Makers*, and the National Center for Transgender Equality provides a variety of helpful information. FtM International offers services for female-to-male transsexuals and their families. There is an organization based in England, called Mermaids, for transgender children and their families.

There are several annual transgender conferences. The largest and, I believe, most informative, is the Philadelphia Trans Health Conference. Its scope has grown from the original focus on health issues of special importance for trans people to encompass a broad range of workshops and presentations on many facets of the transgender community. I have been particularly impressed by the development of a broad selection of workshops related to spirituality of one form or another. The conference even offers facilities for children, making attendance by an entire family feasible and rewarding.

Virtually all of the resources I have discussed here have a presence on the Internet, which has had a tremendous impact on communication within the trans community. It is also a great source of trans-related material for families, friends, spouses, and the general public. There are innumerable relevant websites, including some offering support directly to trans children and adolescents. I would encourage parents to search the Internet for any trans-related subject they are interested in learning about and for forums and LISTSERVs that can put them in touch with other parents. The only one that I will mention here is called Transgender Forum, which includes continual coverage of trans-related news items.

As useful as all these resources can be, ultimately your most important resources are your own love for your transsexual child, your commitment to his or her well-being, and your determination to do everything you can to provide a safe, loving, and encouraging environment for him or her to grow up in. He or she will face certain challenges in life because of being different, but your love, support, and understanding will prepare him or her to meet those challenges successfully. You may be surprised, confused, and even disappointed when you first become aware that your child's gender is not what you had every right to expect, but he or she is the same child you always had and needs your love and support more than ever. And because your child *is* your child, you will be there for him or her, and his or her future will be bright.

RESOURCES

Publications

Welcoming Our Trans Family and Friends. Parents, Families and Friends of Lesbians and Gays (PFLAG). http://community.pflag.org.

Our Trans Loved Ones. PFLAG. http://community.pflag.org.

Standards of Care for the Health of Transsexual, Transgender, and Gender Nonconforming People. The World Professional Association for Transgender Health. http://www.wpath.org.

Transgender Equality: A Handbook for Activists and Policy Makers. The National Gay and Lesbian Task Force. http://www.thetaskforce.org.

Organizations

National Center for Transgender Equality. http://transequality.org. Provides a variety of helpful information, including a transgender terminology document.

FtM International. http://www.ftmi.org. Offers services for female-to-male transsexuals and their families.

Philadelphia Trans Health Conference. http://www.trans-health.org. The largest annual transgender conference, offering workshops and presentations on many facets of transgender life, including a spirituality track.

Transfaith Online. http://www.transfaithonline.org. The first web-based transgender community with an interfaith spiritual perspective.

United Methodist Alliance for Transgender Inclusion (UMATI). https://www.rmnetwork.org/newrmn/connect/extension-ministries/united-methodist-alliance-for-transgen-der-inclusion-umati/#! An extension ministry of the Reconciling Ministries Network, with an active Facebook group.

Mermaids (UK). http://www.mermaidsuk.org.uk. Support services for transgender children, teenagers, and their families.

Trans Student Educational Resources. http://www.transstu-dent.org. Dedicated to making schools and colleges more accommodating to the needs of transgender and gender nonconforming students.

Trans Youth Family Allies. http://www.imatyfa.org. Offers a very wide range of resources for children, teenagers, and parents.

Gender Spectrum. https://www.genderspectrum.org. Helping to create gender sensitive and inclusive environments for all children and teenagers.